Set Your Sights on Success

TIME LIFE BOOKS

MINDPOWER
JOURNEY THROUGH THE MIND AND BODY
COOKERY AROUND THE WORLD
LOST CIVILIZATIONS
THE ILLUSTRATED LIBRARY OF THE EARTH
SYSTEM EARTH
LIBRARY OF CURIOUS AND UNUSUAL FACTS
BUILDING BLOCKS
A CHILD'S FIRST LIBRARY OF LEARNING
VOYAGE THROUGH THE UNIVERSE
THE THIRD REICH
MYSTERIES OF THE UNKNOWN
TIME-LIFE HISTORY OF THE WORLD
FITNESS, HEALTH & NUTRITION
HEALTHY HOME COOKING
UNDERSTANDING COMPUTERS
THE ENCHANTED WORLD
LIBRARY OF NATIONS
PLANET EARTH
THE GOOD COOK
THE WORLD'S WILD PLACES

M Í N D P O W E R

Set Your Sights on Success

TIME-LIFE BOOKS
Amsterdam

MINDPOWER

Created, edited, and designed by DK Direct Limited,
Brookmount House, 62-65 Chandos Place, London WC2N 4HS

A DORLING KINDERSLEY BOOK

DK DIRECT LIMITED

Series Editor Luci Collings
Deputy Series Editor Sue Leonard
Senior Editor Lee Stacy
Editors Fran Baines, Sue George, Ann Kay

Managing Art Editor Ruth Shane
Designers Sam Scarborough, Becky Willis

Publisher Jonathan Reed
Editorial Director Reg Grant
Design Director Tony Foo
Production Manager Ian Paton

Editorial Consultant Keren Smedley
Contributors Vida Adamoli, Claire Calman, Victoria Davenport, Sue George, Patricia Spungin-Cook

Editorial Researcher L. Brooke
Indexer Ella Skene

TIME-LIFE BOOKS EUROPEAN EDITION
Staff for Set Your Sights on Success

Editorial Manager Christine Noble
Editorial Assistant Mark Stephenson
Design Director Mary Staples
Designer Dawn McGinn
Editorial Production Justina Cox
European edition edited by Tim Cooke

First Time-Life European English language edition 1996
ISBN 0 7054 1634 8
TIME-LIFE is a trademark of Time-Warner Inc., U.S.A.

Printed by GEA, Milan, and bound by GEP, Cremona, Italy

30 29 28 27 26 25 24 23 22 21 20 19 18 17 16 15 14 13 12 11 10 9 8 7 6 5 4 3 2 1

CONTENTS

INTRODUCTION

SUCCESS MEANS DIFFERENT things to different people. For some it is the accumulation of wealth or the realization of a dream. For others it might be career advancement, the achievement of long-standing ambitions, or establishing a secure and happy family. And there are those who would say that the most valuable success of all is to become a wiser, kinder, and more fulfilled human being. In essence, however, all types of success can be thought of in the same way: the attainment of something you set out to achieve.

What's important to you

To be successful on your own terms you must first decide what success means to *you*, to your own circumstances and aspirations. In this book, you will be encouraged to look at various aspects of your life, and to judge for yourself what matters most to you. Is your idea of success a demanding job that makes the most of your talents, or is it a large, comfortable home and a happy family life—or both of these, perhaps? If you had to choose, what sort of goals would you commit yourself to: financial rewards or personal growth? When you have discovered what is most important to you, then you will know how to set about tackling the many issues and challenges that are bound to arise in your quest to be successful.

Playing your cards

Fate, it is said, deals the cards and Determination decides how you play them. Everyone knows someone who seemed destined for success yet somehow never managed to accomplish anything. On the other hand, there are those with every conceivable disadvantage in life who go on to achieve great things. The truth is that some people squander every opportunity that presents itself or, worse still, actually fail to recognize that the opportunity is there—and many of us do a bit of both. People who have truly successful lives not only make good use of the opportunities that life throws at them, but are able to turn almost everything—including setbacks—to their advantage.

In order to play your own personal deck of cards effectively—and the reality is that some people are dealt a much better hand than others—you must recognize your abilities and put them to full use. You must also take responsibility for the realization of your dreams, however hard or unlikely it might

Reach for the stars

One of the secrets of success is aiming high, and not settling for less than you want. To achieve this you first need to decide exactly what success means to you; then you must commit yourself to achieving it.

seem to you at present. Ultimately, success is a choice like any other. As countless individuals from every walk of life prove each day, success does not come gift wrapped with the morning post. Rather it is something that you make happen through effort, persistence, and determination.

Making it happen

Everyone is born with the potential to succeed, but much of that potential never gets used. Fear, self-doubt, procrastination, and laziness all conspire to limit our horizons, and we often find it much easier to list all the things we can't do, rather than those we can. Although potential might get rusty from neglect, it doesn't disappear. Regardless of what sort of education we've had, the encouragement—or lack of it—we received from parents and teachers, and the knocks we've taken along the way, our potential is still there, waiting to be discovered or re-awakened. What each of us has to learn is how to realize this potential.

Action stations

If you remain a passive onlooker, then life is likely to pass you by. Once you begin to take an active interest in your own destiny, however, you may find that a whole chain of new and unexpected events is set in motion. You may be surprised at how suddenly everything comes together to help set you on your path to success.

Every journey starts with a single step. The first step on the road to success is to understand that it is not the world that is holding you back, but your lack of belief in yourself. The next is to take the appropriate action and develop the necessary skills to get you where you want to be. Exactly how you do this will depend on what you are aiming for, and as you work your way through this book, you will find various means of developing the resources you will need to get ahead.

The most important thing you have to do is to commit yourself to your goals, whether small or large, short- or long-term. Once you have done this, you are on your way to making your dreams become reality. As the German poet and dramatist Goethe put it: "Whatever you can do, or think you can, begin it. Boldness has genius, power, and magic in it. Begin it now."

SUCCESS AND THE PERSON

Success comes to different people in different ways. Take James, for instance, a child prodigy who gave his first public performance on the piano at the age of seven. At the age of 14, despite the hesitancy of his parents, who wanted him to have a normal childhood, he was giving recitals throughout Europe and the States. At 17 he started composing, and when he was 20, the London Philharmonic Orchestra performed his first symphonic work. Today, he is in constant demand throughout the world, as both a soloist and composer, and his musical engagements are booked up years in advance.

Success through adversity

Cathy, on the other hand, married at 17 and for the following 15 years was the victim of persistent domestic violence. When she and her two teenage sons eventually escaped her abusive husband, all she took with her was a fierce determination to do something of value with the rest of her life. By day, Cathy worked as a cleaner and at night studied to be a teacher—an exhausting process, which she sometimes found difficult to sustain. It took her seven years but she finally made it. Her first post was at an elementary school and she is still there. Although it's in a deprived inner-city area—and the school's problems reflect that—Cathy's enthusiasm for her work inspires and sustains her and her pupils. As she says, "What you give in life is every bit as important as what you get."

With James, his dazzling talent—combined with persistence and commitment from a young age—led to his success. In Cathy's case it was partly through adverse circumstances that she developed the qualities she needed to make her life a success. What they both have in common, however, is achievement in the field that is most important to them.

Different aspects of success

Success means different things to different people, and as such reflects the whole spectrum and scale of human desires. Breaking the habit of biting your nails is a success, for example, as is saving a small sum of money each month, sticking to a diet, or learning to drive a car. Some successes have larger implications for those who achieve them, of course—getting an important promotion, masterminding a boardroom takeover, or being elected to public office may lead to profound and long-term changes in your life which you had not anticipated.

Some very worthwhile successes are a direct result of coming to terms with failure elsewhere in life, as in the case of the dancer who accepts that he or she actually lacks the special talent to become a soloist and retrains to become a choreographer instead; the man who realizes he'll never make a professional football player, who then channels his love of the sport into coaching; or the woman who discovers she cannot have children so she becomes a foster mother, helping the underprivileged children in her care through her love and commitment.

The many faces of success
To everyone, success means something different, and will mean different things at different times in your life.

Changes

When young, many people are convinced that life will give them everything they long for: money, fame, everlasting love—the lot! As people grow older, however, they come to realize that this is not how the real world works. Prince or pauper, wise man or fool, magnate or underling, nobody is ever

successful in all things at all times. Furthermore, the successes people aspire to change and develop with experience and the passage of time.

For example, take Becky, whose ambitions and how she viewed success changed markedly as she grew up. When she was a plump 14-year-old all she wanted was to look like a Hollywood movie star and to attract the attentions of the guy who lived across the street. A few years later, thinner and more glamorous, Becky turned her attentions toward gaining a degree. However, the social whirl came first until her last year, when her desire for academic success took over. A good degree under her belt, she focused on her career—which took five hard years to get going. At 28 she was working in educational publishing and had been living with her boyfriend in a rented apartment for five years. Her goals were to become editor, marry her boyfriend, and buy a house. She got the promotion and the house, but her relationship collapsed. At 33, a good relationship is her top priority.

Be realistic

Each one of us is a unique individual. Our combination of personality, inherent ability, and interests make us more suited to certain activities than others. A person with a natural flair for dealing with people, say, will feel frustrated in an occupation that requires him or her to work in complete isolation. Equally, for a logical and analytical thinker, a job which demands quick-fire, creative ideas would force the person to go against his or her natural grain. Some people are aware of their talents from childhood, others discover them almost by chance in adult life; many need help to find them, and after they have done so are surprised, because they seem so obvious! Whenever it is that you discover your own talents, however, the important thing is that you make good use of them. For it is by harnessing your abilities to your objectives that you become more successful. Whatever your talents, it is important that you are honest with yourself about them. However much you may dream of being an opera singer, for instance, there is no way you are going to find yourself on stage at the famous La Scala opera house in Milan unless you possess a naturally spectacular voice.

Achievement

It is essential to set realistic goals, and add markers to know when you have achieved them, so that you will know when you can move on to something else. Remember, however, that consistent success rarely comes about without sustained effort. Whatever areas you want to achieve in—health, relationships, study, family, social life, sport, community, money-making, creativity, and so on—you have to pursue your own goals with focused energy and persistence.

It is also important to acknowledge the successes—even the smallest and most personal—that we do achieve. The esteemed American writer F. Scott Fitzgerald was haunted by chronic discontent, despite being a great social and literary success. A friend of his from youth said of the writer, "I felt that he was one of those people who could never be satisfied with life. He seemed to feel there must be something more that he hadn't gotten and could never get."

Although it is appropriate to set new goals once you have achieved one lot, dissatisfaction that gnaws away at every achievement and makes you feel that you are forever missing out will never make you successful. Instead, you need to congratulate yourself for what you have done and feel proud of all your achievements, whether large or small.

What Does Success Mean to You?

Do you know what success really means to you? Read through the following sections to figure out which category best reflects the sort of success that you most admire—influential, financial, relationship, or personal. Each section gives three different examples of people who are outstandingly successful in one area of their lives: the people with whom you identify the most will indicate the area where your aspirations currently lie. This introductory article is designed to be thought-provoking, to make you think about how you have viewed success until now. However, as you work your way through this book, you may find—because it addresses many different aspects of success—that you reevaluate what you think success is.

Status?
Do you place power and influence above everything?

Influential success

• Janet is single and the fashion editor of a popular women's weekly. She attends all the big fashion shows and socializes with top models and designers. Her influence has been considerably increased by the fashion column she recently started writing for a Sunday newspaper.

• Peter is an internationally famous performer of rock music and the world is his oyster. He travels with a permanent entourage of hangers-on dedicated to anticipating his every wish. Wherever he goes people trip over themselves to do his bidding. And whether it is a restaurant's best table, a hotel's largest room, or a fashion designer's latest outfit—he always gets the very best.

• Mark started out as a provincial reporter. At the age of 30 he started a satirical magazine, pillorying politicians and the establishment. It became hugely influential and Mark with it. Recently a prominent politician was forced to resign over financial wrongdoings that Mark was the first to expose.

When you crave power: You are attracted by the power and influence that comes with a certain kind of success. You want to be the one calling all the shots and commanding respect everywhere you go. You are a natural born leader, a general, not one of the troops. Although money is important to you, it is more for the air of authority it bestows rather than what it can buy you. In fact, you would prefer to be poorly remunerated, but firmly in control, than a well-paid lackey.

Financial success

• Louise and Norton are extremely rich jet-setters with a priceless collection of modern and contemporary art that includes several paintings by Picasso. They are also high-profile fund-raisers for various charities, hosting events attended by media stars and royalty from around the world.

• Caroline is a wealthy divorcée with two children at boarding school. She lives in an elegant house, drives a new Jaguar, and takes frequent holidays in exotic places. Most of her time is spent shopping, lunching with friends, and working out at her health club.

• Kevin rose from humble beginnings to become a wealthy international-property tycoon. The highlights of his many grand purchases include a large yacht, a private jet, and a fleet of vintage Rolls Royces.

Possessions?
Many people measure their success by what they have materially.

Relationships?
Some people value family and friends the most.

But his most prestigious holding is the eighteenth-century country estate that boasts a swimming pool and a golf course, as well as a tennis court. His daughter acquired a title when she married the son of an impoverished but well-known English aristocrat.

If money rules: Success to you is wealth and the prestige that comes with it. You desire all the trappings: cars, yachts, designer clothes, and a home beautiful enough to grace the pages of glamorous magazines. For you, possessions are not only delightful, they also symbolize status. For example, you would probably want a tennis court on your grounds even if you never used it!

Relationship success

• Dee is a housewife and mother of three young children. She has a successful marriage based on mutual love and respect. Money is short but neither Dee nor her husband let it get them down. They treasure their children and each other, believing a happy family is more important than anything.

• Karen is a doctor working in Africa. She has formed close ties with members of the local community, who treat her as a friend. It is the quality of these relationships that make the difficulties she has to struggle against worthwhile.

• Mike teaches physical education in a large high school. He takes a special interest in some of the more difficult boys, encouraging them to channel their aggressive energy into sport. He is also a voluntary counselor working with young offenders. With his help many of them are now law-abiding members of society.

When other people matter most: The success you most value is concerned with personal relationships, both with those closest to you and within the wider network of the community in general. You believe that money and influence cannot bring you happiness unless your relationships with others are harmonious and meaningful. A fulfilling partnership, happy, well-adjusted children, and close friendships are of the highest importance, as is contributing to the well-being of those around you.

Personal success

• On his retirement, Anthony decided to fulfill a lifelong dream and study painting. He did a two-year evening course in portraiture. Now a busy artist, he contributes regularly to group shows.

• Pat suffered a nervous breakdown in her mid-20s. She went into therapy and discovered an interest in emotional healing. She went on to train as an art therapist and now works with old people.

• John was an alcoholic for 25 years. He went into recovery after his drinking destroyed his second marriage. Becoming sober was the start of a journey of self-discovery that led him to practicing Buddhism.

Inner harmony?
Personal growth and internal peace is a priority for many.

If you are searching for deeper meaning: Although you might aspire to other types of success, ultimately it is self-knowledge and personal growth that mean the most. You are a seeker after the truth, wanting a philosophy that will make sense of the pain and contradictions of life. To fulfill your potential and achieve inner peace and harmony is your goal.

But What If I Fail?

Whether or not you stand a chance of fulfilling your potential and realizing your goals is, to a large extent, determined by your attitude to failure. High achievers don't expect a smooth ride; they take disappointment in their stride. They know that success does not mean the absence of failure, but the achievement of their ultimate objectives.

Most people experience fear of failure when they push themselves, thinking they might bungle something that means a lot to them. But although this fear is common to everyone, how people respond to it differs enormously. While some people maintain optimism and resolve in the face of obstacles and setbacks because they want to reach their goal, others are so afraid of the prospect of looking inadequate or ridiculous, of exposing themselves to risk and uncertainty, that they simply never try to get on. Most people do not react so dramatically, however—but have some area of their lives where they feel vulnerable and fear takes over.

Experience

In one sense failure is just another word for experience, and experience is the greatest teacher of all. If we recognize this, we can benefit from even the most disastrous events. We can go back over our errors, review the decisions that we made, and examine the way that we handled ourselves and others. The purpose of this is not to wallow in the failure, but to work out a better way of doing things the next time around. In the words of the American golfer Tom Watson, "You learn to win by losing."

This healthy attitude toward failure is one that most successful people share. Although they may encounter the same difficulties as everyone else, they use these experiences to enlarge their understanding.

This was reiterated by American writer Gail Sheehy, who carried out research into "pathfinders" and "complex models for lives truly worth living"—her terms for well-rounded successful people. She found it was their pro-active response to life's difficulties that was central to their achievements. "Pathfinders" turned to helpful coping devices when confronted with disappointment. They threw themselves into work, for example, sought encouragement from friends, and retained a sense of humor.

Coping with fear

People whose fear of failure undermines their lives tend to judge themselves harshly. They constantly put themselves down by saying things like, "I've blown it again." To combat fear of failure, the first step is to replace negative self-talk with a more useful and encouraging script, which means acknowledging each and every success, however small, and telling yourself that you *can* do something, rather than you can't.

Next, act courageously even when you want to run and hide. Generally speaking, people act how they feel—unless socially unacceptable feelings

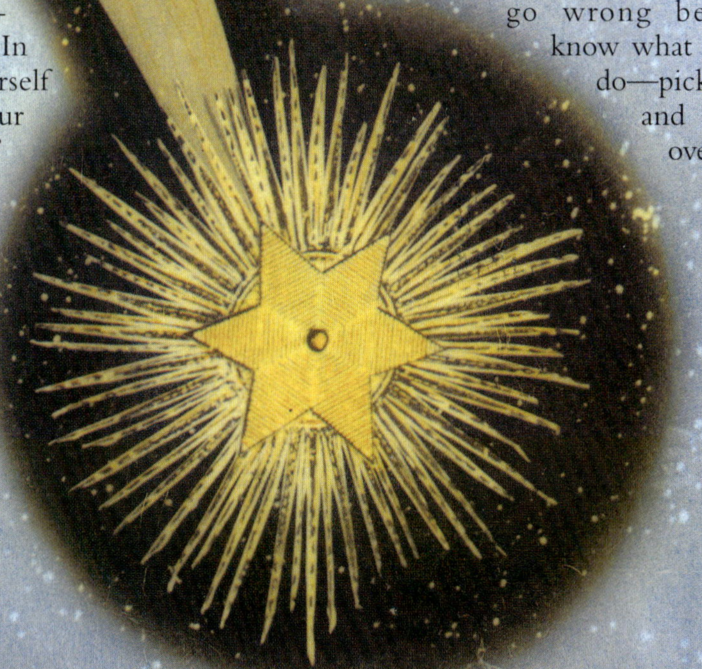

Catch a falling star
Nobody flies high all the time. Once you fall, the key to success is to get straight up again.

such as anger are involved. It is a proven fact, however, that by forcing yourself to behave in a certain way regarding particular circumstances, you can change the way you feel. For example, the skinflint who makes himself give to other people who are less well off will eventually do so out of genuine charity and selfless generosity. In the same way when you force yourself to act courageously, you activate your inner resources and turn "pretend" courage into the real thing. With practice and determination you will develop an image of boldness and self-confidence to replace the old one: passive victim of fear. In the words of the seventeenth-century French general Henri de Turenne: "Of course, I conduct myself like a brave man, but all the time I'm feeling afraid. Naturally, I don't give in to the fear, but say to my body, 'Tremble, old carcass—but walk!' And my body walks."

See things differently

Finding new ways of looking at situations can also help. "Reframing"—changing the meaning of events by looking at them from a different perspective—is often effective. You may also find it useful to use visualization techniques when facing a particularly daunting situation, such as speaking to a large group of people. Being as clear and specific as you can, imagine yourself not only handling the situation effectively, but achieving a spectacular triumph. Now replace this gratifying scene with one that expresses your worst nightmares. The point of this exercise is to establish a sense of proportion; the likelihood is you will neither bring the house down nor suffer humiliating stage fright. The reality will lie somewhere in between where you can cope with it.

Finally, failure is only failure when you don't learn from it. Remind yourself that failure is not fatal, and there isn't a successful person anywhere who hasn't failed at something. So, don't be deterred when things go wrong because you know what you need to do—pick yourself up and then start all over again!

CHAPTER ONE

THE MENTAL CHALLENGE

WHEN YOU DECIDE to aim for a long-cherished goal, it is tempting to rush in and simply deal with each challenge as it crosses your path—your financial situation, a problem at work, or a difficult relationship. But, as this chapter explains, the first, most important, step is to examine your beliefs about yourself and your definition of success.

You will achieve your goals only if you really believe in yourself, so it is important to take an objective look at your life, and become aware of your positive and negative attitudes and how they determine the sort of person you are (see "How Do You View the World?," pp. 18-19). People who are confident have a much greater chance of achieving success, simply because they are less afraid to try things. So, if lack of confidence is your problem, developing a positive mental attitude will help you get more out of life. If you are too negative in your outlook, we show you how to develop and sustain a positive attitude.

In working toward any worthwhile goal, you are bound to come across hurdles, but beware of making excuses for yourself. Many people have overcome extraordinary obstacles—such as poverty or physical disability—and achieved great things, proving the amazing power and determination of the human spirit.

It is important to be aware that some people are afraid of success (see "Fear of Success," pp. 28-29). This common, yet little-known, emotion is usually a result of low self-esteem. Fear of responsibility, fear of failure, or even the feeling you don't deserve to succeed are all symptoms of this problem. Another emotion that holds people back is fear of change. But this fear can also be turned round, enabling you to welcome change as the door to a world of exciting opportunities.

There are many techniques that can make it easier for you to stick to your challenge. One idea examined in this chapter is Maslow's theory of self-actualization, which is structured around recognizing and building on your positive potential. There are also exercises, such as creative visualization, described on pages 34-37, that can help you to focus on your goals.

By building on the positive and overcoming your doubts and fears you will really begin to believe that you can achieve your goals and realize your dreams. Once you have done this, you will find it easy to convince the rest of the world of your abilities.

SUCCESS IS A STATE OF MIND—IN ORDER TO REACH YOUR GOALS YOU MUST FIRST CONVINCE YOURSELF THAT YOU ARE CAPABLE OF ACHIEVING THEM.

A QUESTION OF ATTITUDE

WHATEVER YOUR CHOSEN PATH, the journey toward success begins in your mind. The reason for this is that your life is a reflection of your attitudes and beliefs. How you behave—and how others behave toward you—is strongly affected by your personal philosophy. People who are convinced that the world is a cut-throat jungle, for instance, will manifest this belief in aggressive behavior; those who believe that treating people with compassion brings out the best in them will behave accordingly. Also, individuals who value themselves expect to receive respect from others, and this expectation tends to be fulfilled. It follows then that your attitudes ultimately control much of your experience of the world.

Your own character and personality are affected by your attitudes in exactly the same way: the image you have of yourself—as attractive, strong, ineffectual, creative—is what you will ultimately become. You are the master of your fate because your fate is controlled by your attitude, and if your attitude is pessimistic and self-defeating, then you can never achieve success. A positive attitude, on the other hand, not only allows you to make the most of any opportunities that arise, it also acts as a powerful magnet, attracting a wide range of life-enhancing people and situations.

The positive charge

The English poet John Milton asserted that, "The mind is its own place and in itself can make a Heav'n of Hell, a Hell of Heav'n." In their book *Success Through a Positive Mental Attitude*, Napoleon Hill and W. Clement Stone communicate a similar message—that we can revolutionize our lives by changing the way we think. According to Hill and Stone, each of us has an internal talisman, on one side of which is written PMA (Positive Mental Attitude), and on the other NMA (Negative Mental Attitude). PMA is the quality that enables some of us to achieve success. NMA has the opposite effect—it leads to defeat, resentment, and discontent and, left unchecked, it will stop you from fulfilling your potential.

It's how you view it

Life, like a hand of cards, can be played with a positive or negative attitude, affecting, among other things, how people respond to you.

For some people, facing every situation with PMA is a manifestation of the inner confidence and optimism that comes from growing up in a secure, loving environment. Others manage to summon PMA when things are going well, but switch back into NMA the moment they encounter a problem or a setback. The secret of achieving real success, however, is sustained PMA.

The first step in transforming negative attitudes into positive ones is accepting responsibility for your life. In the face of failure or disappointment, the classic NMA response is to place the blame elsewhere: "I never went to university," "My parents didn't believe in me," "I'm a victim of the class system," and so on. The much more serious handicap in all these cases, of course, is the negativity behind them. Not only do these attitudes fuel defeatism and low self-esteem, they also amount to burning bridges before they are even in sight.

Turning your life around

Turning NMA into PMA means accepting that if you want to change your life, the place to start is with yourself. Every time that you feel a negative attitude surfacing, try to stifle it, and then replace the negative attitude with a self-affirming message such as, "I know I can do this," or "I deserve this." You may be surprised at how habit-forming your negative reflexes have become.

Another effective technique is to identify with someone you admire—a friend, perhaps, a respected teacher or colleague, a public figure, or even a character from fiction—and try to imagine how that person would behave in a particular situation. A teenager, for example, might deal with a gang of bullies by mustering the courage of a favorite fictional detective. In the same way, you could find the inspiration and courage to tackle difficult situations by reacting in the style of your own role model.

Eventually, this "borrowing" of someone else's optimism and confidence has a good chance of producing the desired result—a Positive Mental Attitude that is instinctively and consistently your own.

PRINCIPLES OF SUCCESS

Remarkably successful people tend to have certain specific traits in common. It is worth noting that Positive Mental Attitude is an important and essential factor in all of these traits, among which are:

- Clarity of purpose—knowing precisely what you want to achieve—and self-discipline; doing things that have to be done even when you would rather not.
- Focused attention—the knack of concentrating on a single issue.

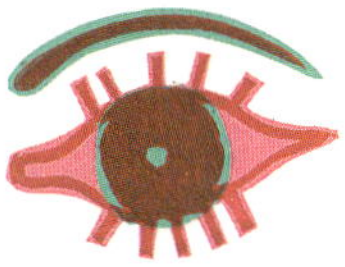

- Willingness to do more than strictly necessary, such as putting in extra hours, experimenting with alternative ways of doing things, and so on.
- Imagination—the power to visualize how things might be.

- Good physical and mental health.
- Basing decisions on sound logic and correct information, while not ignoring or compromising your own set of beliefs or standards.

- A strong determination to succeed, and the ability to experience and communicate genuine excitement.
- Effective use of time and money.

- The potential to learn from failure, disappointments, and set-backs.
- A pleasant personality, and the capacity to inspire respect and affection in others.

How Do You View the World?

Each of us views the world through a very personal and unique pair of "spectacles," which affect how we perceive everything that happens in our lives. The lenses are tinted by our basic temperament, our experiences, and our opinions—and how we have been brought up colors all of these. Here are five scenarios for which you are asked to choose the interpretation that seems closest to how you would react or feel. Then have a look at the conclusions at the end of page 19.

A new boss

The directors of the manufacturing company where you work surprises everyone by appointing an extremely young woman to the new position of planning manager. You discover that she has never worked in industry before. She is responsible for ten people, of whom you will be one. Do you:

a) Suspect that she must have used family connections to get chosen over the other candidates. You are convinced that she will be less able than her predecessor and worry that her lack of competence will make your own job more difficult.

b) View her appointment as yet another sign that traditions you value, such as promoting people within the company after some years of service, are being undermined. Furthermore, you expect that she will be an ambitious, pushy person with impressive academic qualifications but little "hands-on" experience. You prepare to fight her every inch of the way.

c) See her appointment as important as far as letting fresh air into the company goes. You intend to be fully cooperative, reserving judgment on her ability and skills until she has had time to prove herself.

d) Think it's great to give such a young woman a chance. You expect only good and positive things to come of it.

Are they louts?

It is a beautiful summer's day and you are enjoying the sunshine in your local park. After a while, three young men arrive and sprawl out on the grass near where you are sitting. They wear badly torn, dirty jeans and multiple earrings, one has a shaven head, and they are talking and laughing loudly. Do you:

a) Feel immediately unnerved and threatened by their presence. Everything about them confirms your fear that nowadays it just isn't safe to spend any time in public places on your own.

b) Feel outraged that you can't enjoy the simple pleasure of sitting in a park without louts arriving to spoil it. Every fiber of your being tenses as you wait for them to start behaving badly.

c) Remind yourself that you can't judge a book by its cover. You hope that they have come to enjoy the park like everyone else, and just wish that they would pipe down a bit.

d) See three healthy young lads having fun. It is a beautiful day and all you can think of is how delightful life is when the sun shines.

What are they doing?

You are out walking in a stretch of countryside that you know like the back of your hand. Suddenly, you see a car pull up ahead and hear quite loud music drifting out of its windows. The car starts to make its way slowly down a rough track that you know is private property. Do you:

a) Assume that this is a car load of ignorant city-dwellers who have absolutely no respect for, or knowledge of, the countryside, but walk on in case something more sinister is afoot.

b) Feel that this is yet another sign that no one is capable of mapping out a proper route or of respecting other people's property. You run to tell them they are trespassing.

c) Wonder what is going on and whether you can help. Is the driver lost—

this is a poorly signposted area—or having a spot of car trouble? Are these friends or relations of the people who live a mile or so down the track? You gather pace in case you can be of any assistance.

d) Feel glad that this happy bunch of people are having a nice day out enjoying the countryside and think no more about it.

Noisy neighbors

You hear that the apartment downstairs has finally been bought and eagerly wait to see who your new neighbors are. Over the next few weeks, you hear signs of life downstairs, but no one comes to introduce themselves. You see a whole variety of people come and go, at all times of the day and night, but when you pass any of them and smile, they show no desire to stop and chat. Do you:

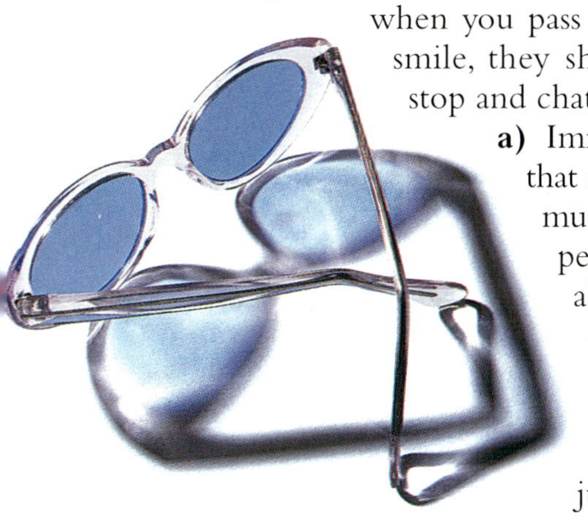

a) Immediately assume that something strange must be going on—perhaps this is actually a cover for a drugs operation.

b) Feel annoyed that you, of all people, can't just have ordinary neighbors, and go and ring their bell on some pretext to see if you can take a closer look at what might be going on.

c) Weigh up the other options. This may simply be a group of friends or an extended family who keep unconventional hours, perhaps because they are shift-workers. Just because they aren't a "9-to-5" nuclear family doesn't mean that they are a bunch of criminals. However, your curiosity is aroused, and you keep a fairly close look-out.

d) Assume they are people who like partying, retiring late, and having lots of friends to stay over.

Was it violence?

You are in a restaurant and notice that the man and woman at the table next to you are having a very heated argument. The woman, who is facing you, has a black eye. Do you:

a) Immediately assume that the woman has been hit by the man and that this is probably not the first time it has happened. The scene shows just how violent contemporary society is becoming.

b) Feel angry that any man could hit a woman. You become so outraged that you believe it is your responsibility to defend the woman.

c) Recognize that the couple's body language reads more like a disagreement—the sort that all couples experience periodically—rather than a violent episode. You admit that the woman's black eye is disturbing, but acknowledge that there are numerous accidental ways she might have got it.

d) Fail even to consider the implications of the black eye and simply find the scene rather exciting. You hope it escalates to a dramatic climax before you finish your meal.

What kind of spectacles do you wear?

Human response to situations is wide-ranging, complex, and influenced by an individual's mood, so this analysis is only a very general indication of your character and viewpoint.

Mostly As: You tend to be anxious and fearful, liking the security of familiar things and suspicious of change. You believe that your life and society are run by a powerful few, or Fate, and there is not much the ordinary person can do about it.

Mostly Bs: You harbor a lot of aggression and expect to have to fight for what you want—be it a job, a relationship, or simply a parking space. You can be a loyal and powerful force where a worthwhile cause is concerned, but the reverse side of this coin is your dogmatism and inflexibility.

Mostly Cs: You are confident, fair-minded, and look at the facts before jumping to conclusions. You dislike any form of bigotry and believe that many of society's problems could be avoided if people would just try to communicate effectively.

Mostly Ds: Your relentless optimism borders on naivety, and is often rather uncaring of other people's deeper feelings and welfare. You don't like facing life's harsher realities—when the news is bad, for example, you simply don't read it.

Be All That You Can Be

The experience of being and doing all you can is something to strive toward because most people are always capable of achieving more. This process of developing as a person—culminating in what is known as self-actualization—involves increased psychological health, personal growth and fulfillment, and, ultimately, greater happiness. Self-actualization is not limited to a few highly creative and successful people; anyone with the right attitude and commitment can learn to achieve it.

Your personal pathway to success
According to Maslow, you carry elements of both your past and future within you.

Maslow's hierarchy

The concept of self-actualization was devised by psychologist Abraham Maslow. He stated that humans have a hierarchy of six levels of need (see below), wherein the lower ones must be largely satisfied before the higher levels can be tackled. The first, primitive needs are present at birth, while the higher needs develop later.

The first four needs Maslow called "deficiency needs" because it is possible to satisfy them to the point that they are no longer problematic. For example, if you feel hungry you can eat until your hunger is satisfied. Those who are really hungry, however, will be unable to concentrate on anything else until they have been fed.

The two highest needs—self-actualization and transpersonal—Maslow called "being needs," since in seeking to satisfy them, people enrich their being. For example, learning to appreciate music stimulates a desire to know more. The other "being" need, transpersonal need, is about how individuals can contribute to the well-being of humanity.

Maslow believed that it is in satisfying these higher needs that human beings reach the full flowering of their special talents and unique abilities. The following are examples of self-actualization:

- An artist gets a "high" from her conviction that in a particular piece, everything about it has worked out just right.
- A lawyer, wading through the evidence in a tricky case, gets a "Eureka!" feeling when he cracks it.
- Putting the final touches to his decorating schemes, a homeowner gets real pleasure from the way the rooms have "come together."

Maslow's Hierarchy of Needs

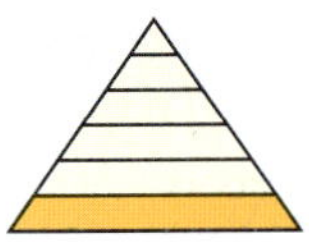

Physiological needs. Food, water, warmth, sex, and physical contact are the most basic survival needs. Unless they are met, they can totally dominate all other forms of behavior.

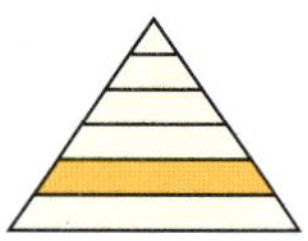

Safety needs. At this level, we must feel free from threats to life and health. Safety needs also include a secure home, regular routines, and familiarity with the world around us.

Need for belonging and love. After safety comes love; we need to feel loved by at least one person, and sense that we function in a family, partnership, friendship, or community.

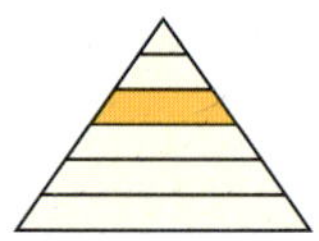

Need for esteem. The next requirement is to feel worthwhile, and know that society values our contribution. The drive to satisfy this need can lead to pursuit of the trappings of success.

Are you self-actualizing?

Consider each of the questions below and mark your answers on a scale of one to five, where five is a strong Yes and one a definite No. Then turn to "Solutions," on page 138, for an analysis of your scores and what your answers mean.

1. Are you frightened of the unfamiliar—whether different experiences or new people?

2. Do you have the ability and confidence to evaluate situations according to your own personal standards, ethics, and needs?

3. Do you have an intolerance for ambiguity and uncertainty in many areas of your life?

4. Can you accept conflict and tension resulting from polarity of ideas and thoughts?

5. Do you feel that life has little that is new to offer; in other words, you've seen it all before?

6. Do you consider yourself to be an expressive person? Are you more natural and less inhibited in your behavior than some of the other people you know?

7. Do you find it difficult to forgive yourself easily when you make mistakes or misjudgments?

8. Do you stick to your own beliefs, regardless of what others think?

9. Are you unwilling to let go of security, such as your parents' financial support?

10. Do you have a strong sense of your own identity? Are you basically happy with yourself?

The richness inside you

In order to be all that you can be, you need to accept and trust yourself, and not be swayed too much by others.

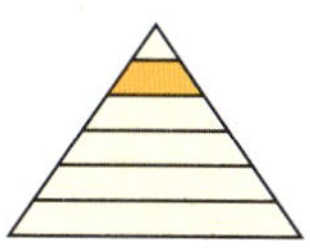

Self-actualization needs. When the other needs have been satisfied, people begin to look for ways to fulfill themselves in creative, intellectual, and interpersonal ways.

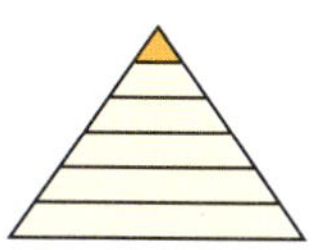

Transpersonal need. Less well-known is the final need to contribute to humanity and feel linked to a spirituality. It is the desire to understand the world and the purpose of life.

THE SUCCESS DRIVE

AMBITION IS ESSENTIAL: without it, you won't have the vision to see how to improve your life or have the energy to make those changes. Whether it's one goal or a more general desire to get all you can out of life, if you want to succeed enough you are halfway there.

Work for your dreams

S. B. Fuller was the son of a black tenant farmer in Louisiana. Unlike other members of their community, Fuller's mother refused to accept that their life of poverty and deprivation was inevitable. "The only reason we're poor is because father has never developed a desire to become rich," she told him. "No one in our family has ever wanted anything better."

These words made an enormous impact on young Fuller. He became a door-to-door soap salesman, putting so much energy into the job that after 12 years he had managed to save $25,000. At this time the company who supplied him came up for sale at $150,000. Fuller put his savings down as deposit and promised to obtain the balance within ten days.

On the eve of the tenth day he was $10,000 short. It was 11:00 p.m. when he drove down Chicago's 61st Street looking for an investor. After a couple of blocks he spotted the glowing window of a contractor's office. Hurrying inside, he explained the situation to the man he found there, promising to pay $1,000 interest on a loan of $10,000. Miraculously the contractor agreed and wrote out the check there and then.

That night S. B. Fuller took the first step to becoming the wealthy man of his dreams. Today he owns controlling interests in the soap manufacturing company, as well as four cosmetic companies, a hosiery company, a label company, and a newspaper.

A burning desire

In their book *Success Through a Positive Mental Attitude*, authors Napoleon Hill and W. Clement Stone used Fuller's story to illustrate how a "burning desire" can overcome seemingly insurmountable obstacles—which in Fuller's case were a deprived home background, little formal education, and racism. He had natural ability and he worked phenomenally hard, but ultimately it was his ambition that got him what he wanted. Fuller had been taught by his mother to believe in the power of personal drive. There was never any question of him giving in. He had committed himself to becoming wealthy, pursuing his goal no matter what.

For "burning desire" we can substitute "ambition" or "success drive"; they are all terms describing the powerful motivation for success. Ambitious individuals stand out in any crowd. They have a forcefulness and stamina that is as much a part of them as the shape of their nose. At their best, they are inspiring examples of what human endeavor can achieve. At their worst, their behavior may be viewed as obsessional and self-centered.

When ambition is essential

Many ambitious people focus very closely on one goal. For professions that demand physical excellence, such as sport and dance, this focus of attention is essential. Roger Bannister, for example, attained his goal of being the first man to run a four-minute mile because it mattered to him more than anything else. He knew that, to achieve the record many thought unobtainable, he had to give everything he had. At the training sessions he pushed himself to the limit of physical endurance and beyond. Nothing distracted him from his purpose until he reached his goal.

Dancers train with the same rigorous dedication, stretching their physical limits in pursuit of their art. Throughout their professional lives they take daily classes to keep their muscles toned and joints flexible. Driven by a burning desire for perfection, they spend countless hours practicing and polishing every move.

Along with inspiration and hard work, ambition is often a necessary part of being an artist. It gives an artist the necessary tunnel vision to focus closely on his or her creation and body of work. For example, a creative writer relies on an ambition to see his or her words and ideas in print. For a performance artist ambition drives him or her toward their goal of seeing their name up in lights and being the object of an audience's thunderous applause. Also, without ambition and self-belief artists would never survive the inevitable rejections and hostile reviews that occur throughout a career.

Creative success
Writers, like all creative artists, need ambition, determination, and dedication to achieve success in their chosen field.

Steps to take

Ambitious people are usually exceptionally vivacious—but everyone can learn how to harness these drives. Being focused on what you want does not have to involve extreme dedication, but can leave enough energy for you to pursue other goals as well.

To achieve success, the first step is to know what you want (see "Making a Life Plan," pp. 76-79). On your way to your goal, bear in mind that success requires you to learn from your failures—this will enable you to harness your positive mental attitudes and direct your energy where you want.

SUCCESS DRIVE AND ADVERSITY

The most inspiring success stories often come from people who have achieved great things despite adversity. Even though you may not have experienced particular hardship in your life, looking at people who have and at how they have turned their lives around will help you see just how much change can be possible.

Many deprived young men have used sport to drag themselves up from poverty, and boxing can boast more rags-to-riches stories than most sports. Legions of young men—especially from black and immigrant communities—have turned themselves into fighting machines for the purpose of pummeling their way out of the economic and social gutter. As any boxing coach will tell you, anger and frustration make for a more ambitious and fearless fighter. What is true of boxing also applies to any sport.

The story of Pelé

In Brazil, soccer is a national passion, particularly so for the legion of ragged boys who not only love the game but dream of becoming soccer stars to escape the slums. Pelé was one such child. Born in 1940 into poverty near São Paolo, he grew up to become arguably the best player in the history of soccer. As children, Pelé and his friends had no money for proper soccer balls, so they improvised and used oranges, tin cans, or balls concocted out of rags and bits of rubber, playing on unsurfaced streets, rugged wasteland, and the beach.

Fighting for success
Many young boxers are from poor neighborhoods, but instead of venting their anger on inappropriate targets, they channel it into winning.

This rough training on difficult terrain honed Pelé's brilliant natural talent. It taught him the superb ball control, mastery, and finesse for which his game became renowned. Pelé played in Brazil's winning team in the 1958, 1962, and 1970 World Cup finals, and enjoyed a career with the New York Cosmos from 1975 to 1977.

Physical challenges

Another adversity that can fire success is physical disability, and some people who face tremendous physical difficulties may achieve things that leave their doctors and relatives astounded. One person who inspired many people with his achievements is Christy Brown, a late-twentieth-century Irish poet who was born with cerebral palsy. His condition was so severe that at the age of five he could not speak or even sit up without support. His fingers twisted and twitched continually, his arms jerked uncontrollably, and his head lolled sideways. He showed no sign of intelligence and everyone—apart from his mother—thought he was mentally retarded. Instinct told her that her son had a working mind. This was confirmed one day when Christy was almost six. Using his left foot, he snatched a piece of chalk from his sister's hand and tried to make a squiggle with it.

Christy's left foot was to become the key to the door of his physical prison. In his autobiography *My Left Foot*, he tells how with the help of his family—and later Dr. Robert Collis—he learned to read, write, paint, and finally type with the toe of his left foot. But overcoming the physical disability that walled him in was just part of his great achievement. With his book about life in Dublin, *Down All the Days*, Christy Brown became a bestselling and critically acclaimed novelist.

Overcoming hardship

Those who have battled their way out of disadvantaged circumstances are often more driven to succeed, in order to ensure deprivation never creeps up on them again. Although their early lives were hard, they had their dreams—and they stuck to them, coming a long way from where they started. One major difference between those who managed to progress and those who did not was the strength of their dreams and their will to achieve them.

Everyone Needs a Dream

You don't have to start from a difficult position to achieve your ambitions. Use these tips to help you visualize your own personal dream, and then harness your success drive to work toward it.

- Have a powerful dream. However far away from it you seem to be at the moment, if you don't have an image of how your life could be, then you won't be able to bring it into being.
- If you find this hard to do, why? If it is because you do not believe that what you want could come true, try and suspend your disbelief. Imagine what you would dream about and aim toward if you believed that your dreams could work.
- Create a clear enough image of your successful life. To achieve all you want, you need to have pictured exactly what it is. This will help you to know the steps and intermediate goals to achieve.
- Think big. Many people do not think big enough: their dreams are small, because that is all they think is achievable. If your dreams are small, then the results will be small too.
- Be motivated so you will be able to direct 100 percent of your energy toward the life you want.
- Take care who you share your dreams with. Negative people will take energy away from your goals, but positive people will encourage you, and may offer practical support.

Light up your dreams
Clear images of what you want in your life, backed up by the motivation to transform them into reality, will give you the best chance of succeeding.

ARE YOU CONFIDENT?

Successful people are confident people, and they often astonish others with the things they achieve. What such people share is a belief in themselves, which—while it does not mean that they will automatically succeed in whatever they try to do—allows them to make the attempt.

By contrast, lack of confidence exacts a high price. It means that you watch opportunities go by without acting on them, feeling that you haven't got what it takes to succeed. However, all is not lost: For many people, confidence does not come automatically, it has to be fostered and developed. Self-belief can be attained by giving yourself consistently positive, not negative, messages. Turn to "Check Your Self-Esteem," on page 98, to help you assess your own level of self-belief.

How would you respond?

To assess your overall level of self-confidence, read the following seven scenarios and in each case, tick the response that you feel would come closest to your own. Then turn to "Solutions," on pages 138-139, to discover your score.

YOU HAVE RECENTLY joined a new company. The boss calls a meeting to discuss attracting business and invites everyone to brainstorm suggestions.

a) You respond by endorsing what someone else has said. You feel your own ideas are weak and that you will look stupid if you voice them.

b) You feel unprepared and panicky. It's only toward the end of the meeting that you manage to come up with a suggestion.

c) You are full of ideas, which you think are good and will help the company. You put them over with enthusiastic assurance.

FRESH OUT OF drama school, you win the leading role in a major, high-profile new play. When it comes to opening night, the production is panned by the critics, and your performance attracts particularly negative reviews.

a) You feel totally devastated and decide that acting is obviously not for you. You are determined never to risk such humiliation again.

b) You suffer agonies of self-doubt but struggle to hang on to your belief in yourself and your interpretation of the role.

c) Convinced of your talent, you are even more determined to survive this setback, learn as much as you can from it, and go on to pursue your original goals of artistic excellence, public recognition, and material success.

A FRIEND TELLS YOU she has just decided to take six months off to travel around India. Armed with a sheaf of brochures, and very excited, she urges you to join her. You have been complaining for ages that your life is humdrum and boring.

a) You immediately come up with a whole string of excuses. But the real reason that you are reluctant to go is that you fear the unknown.

b) You are daunted by the prospect, but realize it could be an enriching and unique experience. You give it serious consideration.

c) You leap at the opportunity and feel as enthusiastic as your friend—you only wonder why you didn't think of the vacation yourself.

A REASONABLY accomplished amateur pianist, you play as often as you can and get a lot of pleasure out of it. A friend is organizing a small concert to raise funds for charity and asks you to take part.

a) You immediately decline. You know you will not have enough time to practice suitable pieces and you can't bear the thought of demonstrating a technique that is less than perfect.

b) Knowing the audience aren't expecting a virtuoso, you resolve to do your best and accept.

c) You leap at the chance to display your skills in public and choose to perform the most challenging composition in your repertoire.

A WELL-PAID GRAPHIC designer, you work on a business publication. Two of your colleagues leave to set up their own design company and invite you to come in with them.

a) Despite the fact that the idea is appealing, you refuse. You find the prospect of the financial and career risks involved too daunting.

b) You are concerned about the loss of a secure salary. After much deliberation, however, you decide to go for it. You encourage yourself with the thought that if nothing is ventured, then nothing can be gained.

c) You feel that your talent and initiative have been restricted for long enough. You agree to join them immediately.

YOU HAVE BEEN in a stable and successful relationship for almost two years. Then one day your partner drops the bombshell that he or she has fallen in love with someone else.

a) Your whole world falls apart. You believe that you are being cast aside because you aren't attractive, sexy, or interesting enough.

b) You are devastated and know that it will take time to come to terms with what has happened. You seek solace from your friends and family, clinging to the belief that you will rebuild your life.

c) You are upset and angry. Telling your partner he or she has lost the best thing that ever happened to them, you start casting around for someone else right away.

YOUR APARTMENT IS shabby and badly in need of minor structural repairs and general redecoration. Although you have no experience of do-it-yourself, cash is short, and your only option is to do the renovation work yourself.

a) You are convinced you would make a terrible botch of the job and resign yourself to waiting until you can afford to call in the professionals.

b) You know you are pretty inept at this point, but decide that anything would be an improvement. You purchase a home-decorating handbook and learn as you go.

c) Your attitude is that if other people can do it, then so can you. You set your sights on nothing less than a complete transformation.

FEAR OF SUCCESS

When a particular challenge seems insurmountable—applying for promotion, perhaps, or taking an important exam—the biggest obstacle is often fear. Fear of failure is familiar to most people, but almost as common and every bit as crippling is the fear of success.

Paul, for example, was very unhappy in his job. The work was boring and solitary, and the salary was low. In the company's monthly staff magazine, he noticed that there was a vacancy for a more-responsible, better-paid position, one that offered day-to-day contact with clients and a considerable increase in pay. He agonized endlessly about the potential move, putting off submitting his application while he discussed the ramifications of the new position at great length with his colleagues, his partner, and many of his friends. In the end, Paul missed the deadline, making the excuse that he was too busy to prepare the required material.

On the surface, it may look as if Paul allowed this opportunity to slip by because he was afraid of being turned down. Actually, the most frightening prospect for him was the strong likelihood that he would actually get the new job. In a management role, Paul realized that he would have to make a wide range of difficult decisions about staffing, budgets, and policy. Also, his relationship with his colleagues would change dramatically. He would be open to criticism from people both above and below him, and any weaknesses in his knowledge, competence, or managerial skills would be exposed. In addition, he would be expected to put in much longer hours, and to function, in the beginning, in an unfamiliar environment.

These and similar concerns are typical for most people who shy away from success. Other common worries center on the effects that a surge in power and prestige might have on close relationships—

A fortress of facts

For some people, studying becomes a barrier against success instead of a means of achieving it.

women particularly tend to be afraid or anxious that their male partners will feel emasculated if they achieve too much in their career. In the same way, some people fear that new-found wealth and status will drive a large wedge between them and their friends, who may feel inferior, patronized, or betrayed by their success.

Ph.D. Syndrome

Some groups of people are particularly prone to this type of fear. Among graduate students, for example, it is so common that the fear has been given a special name: Ph.D. Syndrome. University professors have long been aware of this problem, encountering many especially gifted scholars who do all their course work brilliantly, then do not complete the necessary research or fail to find the required reference sources, or come up with excuses as to why they didn't finish the writing involved in the dissertation that would have earned them their doctorate. In many cases, such students engineer it so that they don't get their degree, and therefore avoid venturing beyond their sheltered academic life. The expectations and responsibilities that outstanding qualifications carry with them are too frightening to cope with. In the end, many such academics become virtually life-long students, gathering an endless assortment of degrees that lead nowhere, or go straight into teaching without ever even applying for a job in their chosen field.

Vanquishing the fear

For those who are paralyzed by the fear of success, the ultimate cautionary tale is the Greek myth of Icarus, who achieved his ambition of flight using wings made of wax and feathers. Ignoring his father's warning, however, Icarus flew so close to the sun that his wings melted, he fell into the Aegean Sea, and drowned. The perceived danger that this myth portrays is clear: ambition is perilous, and the higher the rise, the further and the more damaging the potential fall.

In fact, mistakes, misjudgments, and failures are the price that everyone has to pay for achievement. If you are not able to accept this, you are likely to find some way of opting out whenever opportunities arise. Therefore, repeatedly making excuses for your own inaction—you were too busy, you forgot to take the relevant action, the course/job/relationship was really not right for you, the competition was unfair, and so on—may be a good indication that you are being held back by a fear of success.

If any part of this fear is an honest acknowledgment that you are not equal to a particular challenge, you may be able to enhance your capabilities through study, training, or practice. As in so many other situations, however, the most likely stumbling block is low self-esteem. If, however, you can begin to increase your self-confidence and enhance your self-image, you will be well on the way to conquering your inhibiting, destructive fear of success. To help you assess your true self-image, turn to "Check Your Self-Esteem" on page 98.

WORTHY TO SUCCEED?

In his book *Doing It Now,* Edwin C. Bliss quotes from a survey undertaken by Dr. Martha Friedman, assistant professor of psychiatry at New York Medical College. People who avoided success were asked to complete the sentence, "I don't deserve success because..." The replies that Dr. Friedman received include the following: "Because I lied to get the job." "Because my mother always did my homework for me." "Because I used seduction to get where I am today." "Because I'm lazy." "Because other people deserve it much more than I do." "Because I inherited a lot of money from a relative and consequently I've done nothing to help myself."

These answers reflect a different but equally flawed and damaging reason why some people are reluctant to strive for success—they genuinely believe they don't *deserve* it. Here again, the basic problem is one of self-esteem, and the only way forward is a positive effort to enhance your feelings about yourself.

WELCOMING CHANGE

CHANGE IS A NATURAL law, as inescapable as death. The entire universe—from cosmic dust to planets—is subject to the constant process of change. We live in a world of probability and chance, where absolute certainties do not exist. Even people most persuaded by astrology accept that they cannot know exactly what the future will bring. Although it is human nature to be apprehensive about change, it needn't be feared—in fact it is often a very positive occurance. Viewed optimistically, change can be a welcome, empowering force. As Alfred, Lord Tennyson wrote in his poem "Locksley Hall":

Not in vain the distant beacons. Forward,
forward let us range,
Let the great world spin for ever down the ringing
grooves of change.

Fear of change

The ability to see the positive aspects and possibilities of change is central to leading a successful life. If you respond to change by retreating into a safe little corner, then you will never discover what you might have achieved. If you recognize the opportunity inherent in all change, however, you can use it to move your life productively forward.

For example, Kevin's wife was demanding and ambitious and he had dedicated the past 24 years of their marriage to trying to please her. Then, two days before his 47th birthday, she left him for a younger man with whom she had been having an affair. When the initial shock and distress had abated, Kevin was able to admit that he had been unhappy for years. He could see that he had stayed with his wife, not out of love, but out of fear of the disruption that divorce would bring.

This insight galvanized him into action. He gave up his job as a plumber, stuffed a few clothes into a rucksack, and spent a year traveling throughout Europe trying to "find himself." He picked fruit, worked in restaurants, and gave English lessons to earn money. "The whole experience showed me how fear of change had turned my life into a prison," he says now. "When my wife walked out, she forced

Moving forward
Change is inevitable, whether you have chosen it or not—and it is pointless to try to hold on to the past. Instead, look at the potential that exists for growth and the excitement that awaits you in the future.

change on me. Now, however, I'm the one who's instigating it. What seemed to be a disaster has turned out to be a benefit, and for the first time I'm the one who's in control of my own life."

Finding the positive

Another example of someone who conquered the fear of change is Sharon. Trained in fine arts, Sharon found being a painter too precarious, so she started making loose covers instead. It was an occupation that provided her with a good living. The problem was that she often worked all week and never had time to do any painting. Sharon blamed financial commitments for having to work so hard. The truth was, however, she had become a workaholic for other reasons, too. The precision involved in making loose covers, the fact that nothing was left to chance, made her feel in control of her world.

Having a chest infection diagnosed as emphysema, however, made her face the truth that she was not immortal and that there was more to life than work. She saw that she had dug herself into a safe little hole, refusing to be an artist because of its creative and practical risks. As a result Sharon made a sensible compromise. She cut her workload and gave herself two days a week to paint. As a result, within a year she had sold ten paintings and felt confident enough to become a full-time artist.

Fear of change affects all of us at some time. But, as both Kevin and Sharon show, human beings have a great capacity for survival if they will trust themselves. The novelist Graham Greene once wrote that, "There always comes a moment in time when a door opens and lets the future in." It is up to you to make sure that fear of change does not blind you to that moment when it comes.

Stuck in a Rut?

A consequence of resisting change is that you are likely to wake up one morning and find yourself stuck in a rut. The trouble with a rut is that however unhappy, hemmed in, frustrated, or bored yours makes you feel, it has become as familiar to you as an old pair of slippers. In fact, the thought of exchanging circumstances you know for those you don't sets alarm bells ringing.

In their book *Beating the Comfort Trap*, Dr. Windy Dryden and Jack Gordon describe the typical ruts people get into. They range from a sense of getting nowhere to a feeling of hopelessness and helplessness that borders on depression.

To break out of your rut you have to make a commitment to change by looking at those areas where life has gone stale on you and taking the steps necessary to revitalize them—interrupt your working, TV, and sleeping routine with regular visits to the gym, for example. The emphasis is on action, because only then can you replace unfulfilling patterns and routines with positive ones. As Dryden and Gordon say: "Forever I can sit and stew/But I haven't forever to live and do!"

WHERE TO BEGIN

Castles in the air?
Your ideal goals may not be impossible dreams if you pave your path to them with tenacity and willpower.

Before Roger Bannister ran a mile in under four minutes, most people believed it was physically impossible. After Bannister's achievement, other athletes quickly followed suit and soon a four-minute mile was no longer considered exceptional. It was as if the *conviction* that the fact was impossible actually made it impossible, so that, once the belief changed, others were able to break the barrier, too.

In the sports world, as in other areas, there are individuals who have outstanding ability, but who stop believing that they can and will win—and start losing. Self-belief, tenacity, and willpower are key qualities required for success, and they can be cultivated by anyone for any goal, however great or small. There are all kinds of ways in which you can develop this mind power, and you can find out about some particularly effective ones over the next few pages.

Stepping out

Every journey, no matter how long or complicated, begins with the first step—your personal commitment to a particular goal. Perhaps your first step should be to decide to make a success of your life, and to start as follows:

- Assess where you are now and where you would like to be in one year and five years' time.
- Think carefully about some specific outcomes. For example, rather than simply deciding you would like to be in a better job, you might narrow this down to deciding that you would like to be in a job that uses your ability to deal with people, because you feel that this would make your job seem more of an integral part of your life, and less of a stressful chore that simply gets in the way. You might also like to write down your thoughts in order to clarify them.
- Take a close look at your situation and at yourself. What obstacles are there in your path? Some may be external—for example, you might have to consider moving to get the kind of job you want. Other obstacles may be skill-related—perhaps your desired line of work means you should learn to drive. You also need to work out whether you have the personal qualities required—possibly you need to develop more tact, for example.

Painting an accurate self-portrait

Making an accurate assessment of your talents, strengths, and weaknesses is at the core of reaching your goals. There are three different perceptions of yourself that you should take into consideration:

1. How you see yourself. If you suffer from low self-esteem, you will have a poor image of yourself that will make any kind of success seem out of reach.

2. How you think others see you. If you have low self-esteem, you are certain that others think badly of you, and would think even less of you "if they knew what you were *really* like."

3. How others see you. This is usually something you can only guess at. However, you might try asking your friends to make an honest list of what they see as your strong and weak points. Remember that how you ask for this information will influence the response. Make sure that your friends understand you want a frank assessment. Also, be careful that what you get isn't a self-fulfilling prophecy—if you tend to be something of a "victim," you may ask someone who will give you negative answers.

A self-portrait
In your own mind, what kind of picture do you paint of yourself?

Put these three views together, and write an honest assessment of yourself to form the basis for a self-improvement program. What you think will be affected by your mood, so don't make your assessment in just one evening—take a week or so to complete it.

Pros and cons

Now make a list headed "What I Like About Myself." Give yourself credit for all your positive qualities and skills. Have they all been fully exploited? Then draw up "What I Dislike About Myself." Your third list should be "What I Would Like to Change About Myself," which should include things that are preventing you from reaching your goals. The things that you would like to change should be stated precisely—this makes the task much easier. Jenny, for example, decided she wanted more friends. Then she asked herself what was preventing her from making friends at the moment. The answer was that she lacked confidence to mix with strangers and to initiate friendships. So her new aim became to develop self-confidence and social skills.

What's your image?
Do you sometimes suspect that other people perceive you as being cool, distant, and perhaps even intimidating or arrogant?

Strategies for change

Once you have decided what you want to alter, it might be time for a fourth list: "How I Can Make Changes." One highly effective general technique—visualization—is dealt with on pages 34-37, and this volume explores many other useful tips for change.

One of the most basic things you should do to make appropriate changes is to examine your personal beliefs very closely. Think not only about how you view yourself, but also about how you view the world. Jenny, for instance, might think of herself as a friendless person and believe that little can be done about this. Her attitude would filter through to her actions, making her behave in an awkward, off-putting way. If she created a new "model," she would see how changing her beliefs could affect her actions. Seeing herself as a warm, appealing person, and the world as being full of friendly, interested people, will soon have the effect of attracting others.

As others see you
Find out how others really see you by asking them.

Creative Visualization

We usually recall events by creating pictures in our minds. Think carefully about a recent visit you made to see a friend. Chances are that a whole series of pictures will immediately come flooding into your mind—how your friend was dressed and whether she looked cheerful or sad, what the room you sat and chatted in looked like. But recollections can take many forms other than visual images. Perhaps you will also recall the sounds of the traffic in the street outside your friend's house, the smell and the taste of the meal you shared, and so on. You may feel very strongly as though you are being temporarily transported back to that visit, such is the power of our mental images. Creative visualization is a way of harnessing this power, and making mental images work for us positively in all kinds of ways.

The type of image you conjure up depends on two things:

1. The nature of the recollection. If someone were to say "church bells," your main image would probably be auditory; if they say "roller coaster," you may feel the movement of the ride very strongly.

2. Which of the five senses—sight, sound, touch, smell, and taste—you are especially dependent on or sensitive to. This varies from person to person, and research suggests that people tend to favor one or two senses over the others when it comes to thinking, remembering, and imagining.

Mind over matter

Particularly strong images can affect the body; if you are hungry and you think of fresh bread, your mouth will water. The more vivid the image, the greater the effect. For this link to work in a given situation, there must be a relationship between the two—if you are hungry and think of a rock, nothing will happen.

Not only is your body influenced but so is your behavior. Many of us fill our minds with images of failure before we embark on a course of action, and so program ourselves to fail. If you ask someone out and expect to be turned down, you may ask in a half-hearted way that suggests you are less than great company! Conversely, if your programming says you will succeed, you probably will.

A winning outlook

Since the success of the book *The Inner Game of Tennis* by W. T. Gallwey, athletes have become convinced that the mind plays a huge role in winning. Creative visualization, then, is a major tool, focusing your mind on achieving success by encouraging a positive mental attitude. It has been used to improve:

- efficiency and decision-making in business
- skills, such as driving and using a keyboard
- the quality of relationships
- personality problems, like shyness or aggression

The link between positive images and a successful outcome occurs regardless of whether the image is about a real situation or about a desired one that you conjure up in your imagination—and this is where the strength of creative visualization lies. Imagining yourself coping perfectly well in a highly responsible job will help to promote the calm self-confidence that will spur you on to apply for more senior posts.

The image of success

Although all of us can create images, what is often lacking is the skill to create and hold a clear, strong image, and this is essential for effective visualization. You may have read the theory that the left side of the

Memories and messages

Forgetting to call your partner at an agreed time can cause friction; as a safeguard, imagine a strong visual aide-memoire.

Stepping into your dreams
Your senses play a huge role in visualization—imagining an idyllic beach scene in intricate detail will calm you and help you practice visualization techniques.

brain is responsible for matters of logic and reason, and the right side for creativity. The stress placed on left-brained activities in Western society means the skills associated with imagination need practice.

Before using visualization to help you attain your goals, make sure that those goals are realistic and clearly defined. Also, the goals you set yourself must be of interest and meaningful to you—if you don't really care about them, you can't get involved.

Getting involved

Getting involved is the key to successful visualization. Your images should be as vivid as possible. If you feel you are experiencing the visualization, it is much more likely to enter your subconscious. So, when you visualize yourself living in your ideal house, you must feel *yourself* in that position. It's not enough to look at someone whose house you admire and wish you could change places. You must visualize the feelings and behavior that go with having such a house. Then, look at another person who owns a home you covet and apply NLP (Neuro-Linguistic Programming)—modeling the behavior of the owner until you become like that person. For a further explanation of NLP, see page 41.

There are few rules for what you are visualizing. You may or may not appear in the visualization; you might be looking in on yourself from the outside or feel you are in the middle of it without appearing in person. Your images can be realistic or abstract. For example, instead of imagining yourself in a certain job, you might get as positive a feeling, which you could put to good use, by visualizing something abstract—perhaps an expanse of black changing to bright yellow. There is just one essential: use whatever approach works for you.

USING CREATIVE VISUALIZATION

The great advantage of creative visualization techniques is that they can be done anywhere, at any time. However, in some cases you may find it easier, especially at first, if you have specific visualization sessions. These two pages offer some suggestions as to how you might like to structure such a session. Of course, you can also use any part of the approach outlined here to fit in with where, how, and when you like to conduct your visualizations.

For your visualization session, try to put aside about 20 minutes in a quiet place where you know you will not be disturbed. It helps if you are fully relaxed before you begin. Relaxation is more than just doing nothing. It is a positive state of body and mind, in which you slow everything down and become attuned to your inner self.

There are many different kinds of relaxation techniques and each person should select the method that works best for them. If you have learned yoga or meditation, for example, you might find that they offer effective ways to relax. Many aerobic classes also end with a relaxation routine that you could try copying or adapting. The following are two general methods:

- **Using your muscles.** Progressively tense and then relax the muscles in parts of your body, beginning with your toes and slowly working up your whole body until each and every part is fully relaxed. You could try following this by imagining your body becoming heavy bit by bit—once again, start with your feet until your whole body is in a totally relaxed state.
- **Using deep breathing.** Get into a comfortable position and close your eyes. Breathe in through your nose, and out through your mouth. Place your hands on your ribs so that your fingers just touch in the center. Breathe deeply and feel your rib cage expand and your fingers part. Start to count inside your head—"one" with each breath in, and "two" as you exhale. After a while, your breathing will become shallower and your fingers will remain together.

Get set

Once you are feeling relaxed, move on to the visualization. In the following three visualization exercises—"Picture an object," "Use your imagination," and "Change the past"—you are training your mind and your imagination by working through increasingly challenging kinds of visualization. Once you start to get a feel for the basics, you can begin to apply visualization to the specific areas of your life that you wish to work on. If you have the time to practice every day, then so much the better.

Picture an object

- Take any object—for example, a cup, a vase, or a book. Keeping the object in front of you, study it carefully. Then close your eyes and picture it in your mind. If this proves difficult, start again and persevere until you can do it.
- Once you have mastered the visualization of a single object, move on to a whole room. Take a slow, careful look around the room you are sitting in. Once you've closed your eyes, don't just imagine what the room looks like—imagine its textures, sounds, and atmosphere, and immerse yourself in the experience of being in that room.
- Sit by a window and look out at the scene that lies before you. Visualize the panaroma as it is and then alter it in some way in your mind's eye—imagine how the scene changes at different times of the day and from one season to the next. Experience it, too, with all your senses and emotions.

Use your imagination

- This is similar to the first exercise, but instead of visualizing something in front of you, use your imagination to conjure up images to focus on. For instance, pick an object that is in another room, and visualize it in detail. Now, go and look at it and see if it matches your recollections. Don't worry if you were not absolutely accurate, the important thing is that you visualized it at all.
- Next, visualize a room you know well. Capture all the textures, smells, and colors. Feel the atmosphere and explore the feelings it stirs in you.

Setting the scene

Use every one of your senses when you use creative visualization. Then you will be able to paint a clear picture of the changes you would like to make in your life.

• Now, visualize an imaginary scene in your mind's eye, and then introduce some changes—fill it with crowds of people, introduce some animals, change the weather. You are in charge.

Change the past

• Start by imagining settings and scenes from your past and build up to re-creating specific events. Use your imagination to change the course of what happened. This is not a "What if" exercise but a chance to learn from the past and explore other options.

Now get going

The next step is to use these skills to help bring about changes in your life. Guy is an example of someone who used creative visualization to conquer his fears. He suffered from terrible shyness when it came to dealing with other people socially. In his visualizations, he started off with a brief, casual encounter with an acquaintance. In his mind's eye, he saw how he and the other person were dressed; he saw the park in which they had met; he smelled the flowers and felt the breeze. He saw himself chatting with ease, and felt his companion's positive response.

Guy allowed himself to enjoy the feeling of human warmth, and also to enjoy the satisfaction that comes with pulling off something you find daunting. Next, he talked to a stranger—and when the situation came up for real, found that his mental dress rehearsal stood him in excellent stead.

LV-ABX
TANSA
'S GRAVENHAGE
(THE HAGUE)
HARWICH
ON SEA

CHAPTER TWO

THE MEANING OF SUCCESS

THERE ARE MANY areas of life in which you can strive to be more successful—in your work, home life, or relationships. But these are elements of a rather conventional concept of success. In this chapter a "successful life" is understood to be something broader, and to include elements you might not have considered, such as creative success or success in the family.

Success is a relative and personal concept. In work, for example, we are all slaves to the traditional goals of success, such as promotion or a pay rise. But have you ever stopped to think whether these really are the things that will make you happy? Remember, people want or need very different things from their work. Reevaluating your job by answering some key questions and charting the progress of your career will help you get a clearer picture of what is important to you (see "Charting Your Career Path," pp. 42-43).

In sport—where success is winning, and anything less is failure—many people believe that 80 percent of the challenge is mental rather than physical. Sports psychologists have devised a range of mental techniques, such as centering and visualization, to help athletes focus on their goals, and these can also help people succeed in other areas of life.

There is always the danger that the route to success may appear a bleak and daunting program of mental and physical discipline. But a successful life should be an enriching life, and this chapter also looks at the importance of enhancing your life through learning, and by developing your creative skills (see "Creative Success," pp. 56-57).

Equally, you should not forget that emotional success is just as important as physical and material success. Therefore, you may find it useful to look at your childhood family role, and how it may have influenced your adult behavior. Understanding this may help you build better relationships with your friends as well as your partners. Even though there is no foolproof formula on which to construct your relationships, or choose your partner, in this chapter you will learn some helpful strategies for maintaining and developing a successful relationship in the real world.

Finally, on pages 68-69, there is an examination of the different perceptions of social success. In essence, social success should be measured not by the number of events in your diary, but by the value of those events to you, and the quality of your friendships.

THERE IS NO UNIVERSAL DEFINITION OF SUCCESS. EACH PERSON MUST WORK OUT EXACTLY WHAT IT IS THEY NEED AND WANT, AND HOW THEY CAN ACHIEVE IT.

A Successful Career

DIFFERENT AIMS REQUIRE different strategies. And career success can mean different things to different people. For you, is success about earning a large salary, for example, or having authority over other people? Is it about fulfilling your talents, or having a company car and an expense account? Or is it about feeling that you are doing the very best you can in your job? Once you have answered these questions, ask yourself if you are really on your way to having a successful career.

It's easy to be swayed into thinking that if only you had more—more power, more money, more prestige—you would be happy. We have all grown up with fairy tales of magical, fantasy people who seem to have achieved happiness by slaying the evil dragon. It's no wonder many of us feel that, if only we can achieve that one particular goal, we will have gained everlasting fulfillment. In fact, there are many people who spend years of hard work before they realize that what they thought they wanted doesn't really make them happy at all.

Recognizing real success

Success isn't always what you think it should be. Learning to recognize it when you have it is very important. Many people have worked their way to the top of their career unquestioningly, only to find that they were happier before promotion.

For example, Roger had worked stocking the shelves, helping customers, and taking book orders in a popular bookstore. He had been doing the same job for the past five years and his partner was encouraging him to try something new. When the manager left, Roger decided to apply for the vacancy. Because so many friends had expected Roger to go for the job, he didn't deliberate long before putting his name forward. In light of his reputation as an efficient and conscientious employee he was appointed the new manager.

After a year in the position, Roger admitted that he wasn't happy. He didn't enjoy the change in responsibility, or the hours spent behind a desk plowing through stacks of paperwork. Although he was earning more money, Roger felt he was far more successful before the promotion.

Getting more

If you want more out of your chosen career, one way of starting to do this is to look at the careers of the people you

admire. According to Joseph O'Connor and John Seymour, authors of *Introducing NLP,* everyone can make it to the top simply by emulating the actions of someone successful. NLP (Neuro-Linguistic Programming) is the process of imitating the actions, right down to the speech patterns and mannerisms, of someone you perceive to be successful. By altering any of these inner aspects of yourself, you can make significant changes in your performance and enhance your potential to succeed.

You can begin NLP modeling by carefully observing the person you want to emulate while he or she is actually performing a specific task. For example, you might want to ask your boss if you can sit in on a meeting with an important business client. Focus on your model's general attitude and behavior, and try to work out the reasoning and motivation behind it. To understand these fully, you may have to ask one or two pertinent questions, such as what he or she thought and felt just before making a particularly astute observation, or taking a specific action that you admired.

NLP modeling won't magically turn you into a new person overnight, but with practice it can give you a greater feeling of self-confidence in your ability to perform successfully in your career.

In the end, however, only *you* can decide what success means for you. If your career is simply a means to an end, it is unlikely you will achieve a true sense of fulfillment. If, however, you enjoy your career for its own sake, you have a better chance. Ask yourself: Would I continue to work at my chosen profession if I knew there were no rewards? Your answer should tell you a great deal about what success means to you.

Open the door to success
You need to ensure you are climbing the right ladder to the career you really want.

CHARTING YOUR CAREER PATH

How did you end up in your present job? Was your choice of career affected more by high levels of pay, availability of work, strong family tradition—or merely pure chance? Or did someone point you in a particular direction? In order to move on and realize personal growth, you need to assess why you are doing your particular job, and whether you would like to make any changes.

The right job for you?

The following questions will help you to evaluate your attitude to work—for instance, where you actually started your career, where you are now, and where you want to be—and contribute to an accurate, objective overview of your professional life.

- Is success considered important in your family?
- Were you pressured to succeed when you were a child, either academically or in other ways?
- Have you chosen a career that is similar to that of one of your parents, or something completely different?
- If you could start again, would you have gone into a different profession?
- If the answer is yes, what would you be doing? Would you know how to go about changing to a different career?
- Have you achieved the goals you set for yourself, say, a year ago? Five years ago?

ARE YOU STUCK?

For many people, career success and job satisfaction are elusive. Seduced for the wrong reasons into an unsuitable career, or pushed by well-meaning but misguided parents into a profession for which they have no aptitude, they endure years of misery without taking steps to change it.

It's not always easy to evaluate your own level of job satisfaction; no working life is totally free of frustrations, personality conflicts, and politics. If you dread every Monday morning, however, and you cannot remember the last time you felt really fulfilled at work, you may be stuck in a rut of chronic dissatisfaction known as passive helplessness: the more passive you become, the more helpless you feel you are to change. If you have felt like this for some time, career counseling of some kind may help you regain a sense of control.

Plot your progression

Sometimes it's easier to avoid thinking about the future, because doing so involves first facing the reality of your life as it is now. Often this includes owning up to the fact that you are not achieving or doing what you really want. However, the first step toward change is acknowledging that the present reality does not measure up to your dreams. This could be because your dreams are unrealistic, or your performance at work may be falling short of your potential; if this is the case, try to discover why, and work out what you can do about it.

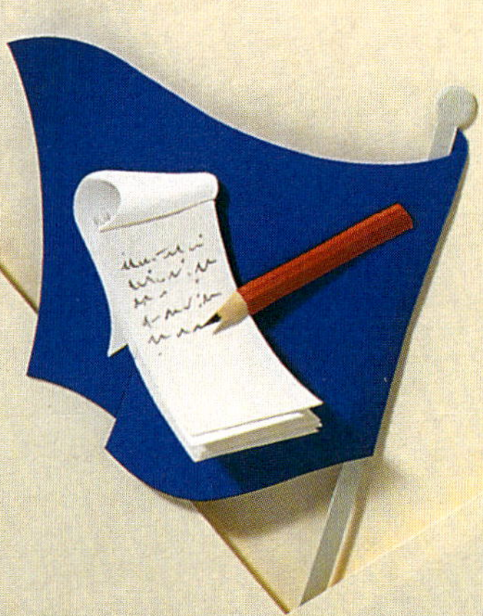

Peaks and troughs

Nancy, who is in her late 30s, made this career graph. Her first job was a fairly menial one making tea, but she enjoyed it. The people she worked with were friendly and she knew the position was only temporary—in the evenings she was taking a secretarial course.

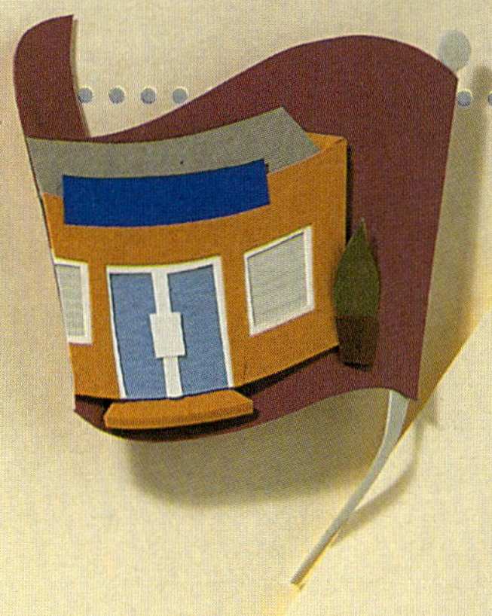

To get an overall picture of your career path, plot it out on a piece of graph paper. Begin by marking the base out in years, starting with your first career step; this could be a job or a course of study. Number the squares along the left-hand edge from one (at the bottom) to 20 to represent the level of success and satisfaction achieved. Plot each of your career moves. For example, you may have felt happy in your first job, (plot 12 or 13), bored several years later (plot 3 or 4), then satisfied again after a promotion (plot 14 or 15). For long periods, your feelings about your job may not have changed.

If your career has followed an uneven path, consider the points at which you were most up and most down. Note that down periods are not necessarily counterproductive; they may indicate times when you were on the brink of change. If your path has risen, your prospects may have been improving even when you felt discouraged. But if it has been descending, you may need to reassess your career—perhaps by answering the questions on these pages.

Finding your niche

As soon as Nancy got her first secretarial job, she realized the work didn't suit her, and asked to be transferred to sales. There, she became fascinated by information technology. This encouraged her to complete a computer course, and she now has her own business creating software for small companies.

- Are you living up to your full potential in general? If you are not, how far below the mark do you feel you really are?
- Do you think your expectations of yourself are realistic? Or are they too high or too low? Do your friends and family agree?
- Are you worried about losing your job? Is this anxiety affecting your performance?
- Are there certain personal characteristics you have that you feel are preventing you from getting ahead—lack of confidence, for example?
- Is there any way you could help yourself to change these things?
- Are there areas of your life that you feel are going well? How could you use these areas to further your career?
- Are you aware of your strengths and weaknesses, not just in your job but also in your life in general?
- Do you think other people are fully aware of your strengths and abilities?
- Where would you like to be in the next year? The next five years? The next ten years?
- Do you feel that the job you are doing now is leading you toward the position you want to achieve in the future?
- If not, what can you do about this?
- If necessary, would you be prepared to change professions completely?

When you have answered these questions, turn to "Making a Life Plan," on pages 76-79. This section will help you set your own career goals, as well as provide advice on how you can take significant steps toward achieving them.

SPORTING SUCCESS

WHAT ACTUALLY GOES on inside a top athlete's mind the day or even the moment immediately before the sporting event? While spectators can see the physical battle taking place on the playing field, track, or court, they are usually completely unaware of the equally powerful mental challenge raging inside the athlete's head. Nowadays in the world of sport, mental conditioning is taken extremely seriously by psychologists, trainers, and coaches, who know that an athlete's overall attitude, as well as his or her mental strength and agility leading up to and during an event, can usually determine the very fine line between winning and losing. As one top sports psychologist has said, "At the level of international competition the difference between two top athletes is usually 20 percent physical and 80 percent mental."

There is a lot that we can learn by examining how professional athletes use their mental and emotional power to cope with the intense pressures of competition, expectation, and failure, as well as success. Many of the mental techniques that are used can also be adapted to almost any area of life in which you might experience performance anxiety, or feel particularly pressured to succeed.

On the track—or in the mind?

The aim of the athlete in competition is to reach a peak at which all of his or her skills are at their sharpest. The athlete must maintain this high point without going over the edge, or pushing him- or herself too hard. To maintain this superior level of performance requires many years of practice and an intense awareness of inner processes.

Most people have experienced the difference between embarking on a venture where they feel convinced that they are going to fail, and going in with a positive state of mind knowing that they will succeed. More often than not, how they are feeling and what they are thinking will dictate the outcome of the event: if, for example, you are feeling negative about yourself and the situation, you will generally fail; on the other hand if you are feeling good about yourself and your capabilities you are more likely to win.

The requirement par excellence for athletes is concentration. For example, tennis players are taught that the most important aspect of the game is to keep their eye on the ball—losing sight of the ball usually means that they will also lose the point. Divers caught off-guard for even a second can ruin their dive. Weightlifters also require intense concentration—imagine what would happen if, having lifted an immense weight over his head, a lifter's concentration faltered. Negative self-talk can also distract, so one coach suggests to his runners that they use portable stereos to listen to relaxation tapes or music to lure them away from any negative thoughts.

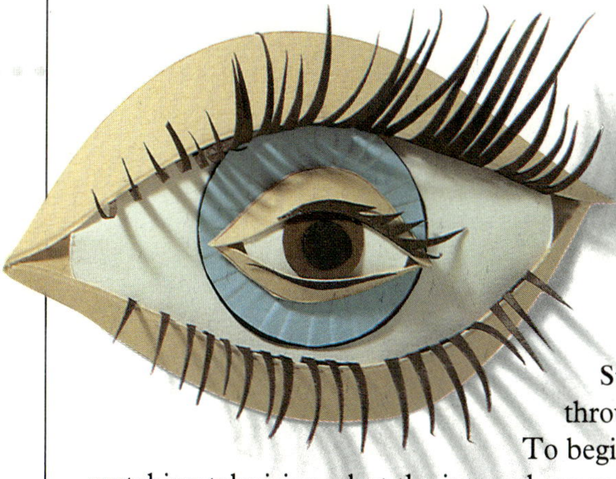

VISUALIZATION

Visualization involves picturing an event in advance, in order to become familiar with it and calm about it. For further information on this see "Creative Visualization," pages 34-37.

Step 1 Sit or lie in a quiet, darkened room. Close your eyes.

Step 2 Spend a few minutes focusing on your breathing.

Step 3 When you begin to visualize the scene, do it in a normal time-frame. Speeding up or slowing down the image isn't helpful.

Step 4 Try to see the event as it would be in real life. Look at it through your own eyes—not as you imagine someone else would view it. To begin with, you may have to use someone else's eyes—for example watching television—but the internal approach has been found to be most successful.

Step 5 Finally, and most importantly, visualize yourself as performing well and in a positive frame of mind.

GOAL SETTING

Concentrating too much on the end result—or winning—can cause you to freeze up and become overly anxious. Try focusing on an inner goal, rather than worrying about winning or losing the big event. Instead of thinking about past records—such as who beat whom when and so on—it's far more constructive to say to yourself, "I'm going to do the very best I am able to do today." This mental attitude moves you away from comparison toward finding inner strength.

Another technique is to surround yourself with as many reminders of your own success as you can lay your hands on—for instance, trophies you have won or photographs of yourself in moments of achievement, as well as remembering in as much detail as possible times when you were successful.

CENTERING

The following technique has been used by Tibetan monks for the past 2,000 years. For many athletes, it is the most common device for mental training. It is particularly useful for when you feel anxious and want to regain control.

Step 1 Stand comfortably and flex your knees slightly. Your feet should be approximately a shoulder-width apart.

Step 2 Relax your neck, arm, and shoulder muscles. Reduce the tension in your jaw by smiling slightly.

Step 3 Concentrate on the movement of your abdominal muscles—notice how they tighten and relax, over and over again.

Step 4 Take a slow deep breath using your diaphragm. Your chest shouldn't move. Do not raise or hunch your shoulders.

Step 5 Exhale very slowly. Feel the whole of your body become heavier as all of your muscles relax.

PERFORMING AT YOUR PEAK

Every athlete, even those at the very top, suffers from an occasional crisis of confidence and periods of crippling self-doubt. For some, this may happen only rarely in the course of a career and is put behind them with comparative ease. For others, however, every fleeting glance at fellow competitors unleashes a swell of anxiety and a complete loss of nerve that makes them feel as if they've failed before they've begun. Such feelings are not the exclusive possession of sportsmen, however, and can happen to anybody. And some of the techniques commonly used by high-achieving athletes to overcome dips in confidence can also be applied equally well to other, non-sporting activities.

Focus your mind

To cope with self-destructive reactions, many sportsmen and women are advised by their coaches to focus on something other than the competitive concepts of success and failure, or winning and losing. Working toward an inner goal rather than gaining victory over one or more opponents can often help you to do this; so make it your immediate goal to surpass your personal best in time or height, for example, or to complete an entire game, race, or circuit without having to lapse into one or more of your most common technical faults.

Another focusing technique that works for many athletes is concentrating on their own breathing. Less structured than centering (see p. 45), this procedure simply involves being totally aware of the sensation of inhaling and then exhaling in a slow, measured rhythm.

Using aggression

There is a clichéd notion that to be a champion you have to be brutishly aggressive. Actually, there is some truth to that. When our bodies are pushed to their physical limit, our minds and emotions react as if we are in danger. This effect is exacerbated by the pressure of competition, which arouses some of our primitive survival instincts. Most athletes become aware that this aggression can be used in a positive way: to sharpen the competitive edge and stimulate the flow of adrenaline which is necessary for running fast, jumping high, or hitting hard. Excessive or uncontrolled aggression or anger, however, can ruin even the most impressive of performances by

---

Lightning strikes

If you are powered by enthusiasm, and then focus it toward your goals, you will be surprised at how much you can achieve.

---

destroying both concentration and control. In addition, repeated displays of temper are considered highly unsportsmanlike, since they are intensely distracting for other athletes—whether they are teammates or opponents.

The first step toward conquering unhealthy aggression is learning to anticipate those situations likely to cause it. Then, when you sense trouble ahead, you can call into play a calming strategy such as centering or focused breathing. Some athletes use what are called "positive self-statements" to reinforce the effect. These are set phrases that address common triggers for anger. If, for example, taunts from opposing players enrage you, try repeating to yourself, "these insults are not personal," or "I will play much better if I keep my temper." Saying these phrases will help you concentrate on your game again.

Serious slumps

While an attack of anger, anxiety, or self-doubt can cause a single failure or a short-term loss of prowess, a much more serious problem for any athlete—particularly the well-known international competitor—is an extended run of poor performances known as a slump. Other symptoms are a general loss of self-confidence, and a feeling of total powerlessness, as if whatever the victim felt he or she was doing right before had disappeared forever. For a committed athlete, an extended slump can cause deep despair and frustration; at its worst, it can even usher in an uncontrollable spiral of slump-failure-slump that signals the end of a career. Clearly, this slide downhill is something that most athletes want to avoid at all costs.

Like other forms of poor performance, slumps are usually the result of specific stress. One of the most common causes is a physical injury of some kind, which then leads to a serious loss of confidence. When this happens, refocusing your energy on some form of remedial exercise will usually lead to increased strength and renewed energy.

The power of the mind

Often, though, an extended slump will have a psychological root, such as the breakdown of a relationship or a bereavement. While sometimes the cause will be obvious, this is by no means always the case, and so to climb out of your slump, you must first look for a method of identifying the source of your stress. One way to do this is by keeping a diary of your moods and worries, alongside a record of your performance. Eventually a pattern may start to emerge that will help you identify the root cause of your problem.

Sometimes feelings may emerge which you can find it hard to deal with on your own. As a result, one increasingly popular way of dealing with such issues is the insight and support offered by counselors who specialize in sports-related problems.

THE RIGHT TRACK

By the time she was 20, Alice was a well-known and successful international sprinter. Her lithe form and easy charm had earned her the love and admiration of thousands of fans. When Alice hit a lengthy slump, her coach, Barbara, was baffled, particularly since Alice had apparently coped so well with the death of her father the previous year.

As Alice's performances faltered, Barbara tried not to let her concern show. Alice herself was depressed and anxious, not wanting to enter events that previously she had won.

In the end, Alice arranged to see a sports psychologist. During their talks, it emerged that her father's death had affected her more than she realized. Alice's father had also been a keen athlete, and much of her drive had been tied up with a desire to make him proud, especially in those events where he had excelled.

When she lost her chance to do this, her ambition had quickly evaporated. With the help of her psychologist, however, she learned to value her achievements for her own sake, and gradually her spirit, and her athletic brilliance, returned.

HEALTH AND SUCCESS

TODAY, MOST PEOPLE ARE AWARE that if they are going to feel better and live longer, then they need to take more exercise and make a change in their eating habits. Despite knowing what it is they should do, however, many people are not willing to make these changes—even if this leads to lack of good health in the long run. This is usually either because they are not willing to make the effort needed to change their current lifestyle, or because they have not fully admitted to themselves that there are measurable benefits to healthy living.

Getting into shape

Your body is a machine that needs to be well cared for and nourished if it's going to work efficiently and as successfully as possible throughout the whole of your lifetime. If you feel tired and edgy because you aren't eating or sleeping properly, it's unlikely that you will be able to enjoy—and excel at—the things that are important to you.

The people who are most successful in the long term are usually those who respect the importance of their bodies and incorporate healthy living into their daily routines. They know that, as tired as they might feel at the end of the day, running in the park or swimming a few laps in the local pool will refresh and revive them, get rid of leftover stress and tension, and give them a head start on tomorrow. They also know eating well now will mean their bodies will repay them with good health later.

Others, unfortunately, find out the hard way. Take Robert, for example, whose case is not that unusual in today's business world. Robert was an ambitious young man who worked in the stock market. While he was aware of the toll the everyday stress was taking on him—he often spent 16 or 18 hours a day in the office, including weekends—he considered it necessary. The fact that he could not sleep, ate irregularly, and drank and smoked excessively bothered him, but not enough to change.

Healthier living

One day, after a sleepless night, Robert began to feel unwell and made an appointment to see his doctor. His doctor was concerned and arranged for a series of tests. When the results showed that Robert's heart was not in good shape, particularly for a man of his age, he became frightened. His doctor told him that only by changing his lifestyle—eating regularly, getting enough sleep, stopping smoking, and getting more exercise, as well as finding effective ways of relieving the stress in his daily life—would he avoid a heart attack. Robert made the effort to change, and in six months his health improved immensely.

A long-term regime for making your body as healthy as possible involves looking at diet, exercise, sleep, and stress management. Incorporate a range of health goals into your life plan and look at practical improvements you would like to make.

Healthy eating is actually very simple, and involves small, regular meals and making sure that you eat a filling, nutritious breakfast each morning. Your daily diet should be low in fats and refined sugars, with a balance of protein and carbohydrate. If you need to lose weight, plan to lose a small amount per week while changing your overall eating habits. Crash dieting should only ever be done under strict medical supervision.

Exercise should also be a regular part of your life: try to get some aerobic exercise, for example, swimming or cycling, for 20 minutes three times a week. Find something you enjoy—you will have a better chance of sticking with it. Irregular sleep patterns are another cause of poor health and low energy. Whenever possible, try to get the same amount of sleep each night, and go to bed and get up at roughly the same time every day.

Be good to yourself

Healthy living should be built into your lifestyle gradually. Don 't make a lot of drastic changes at once, or put too many demands on yourself—like swimming every day if you have never done it before. If you do, you will be setting yourself up to fail. Gain perspectives on what is important and don't be overly hard on yourself if you backslide occasionally. What you do 95 percent of the time is more important than the self-indulgence that may fill the remaining five percent.

You are what you eat
If you change your diet so that it is made up of things that are good for you, you will soon reap the benefit of greater health.

Coping with Stress

Everyone has some degree of stress in their lives—indeed life would be very boring without any stress at all—but some people lead much more stressful lives than others, and it is the way they deal with them that makes the difference. It is a well-recognized fact that people who are hard-driving and put themselves under a lot of pressure to succeed are prone to more stress than their less ambitious neighbors. Not only does the race to succeed lead to an increase in stress and tension, but success itself brings its own stress in terms of increased demands. On the other hand, research shows that people in the upper echelons of business life often suffer substantially less stress than their subordinates, because they tend to have a greater amount of control over what happens in their lives.

A healthy life involves managing stress effectively, so even if you feel fairly calm at the moment, try to build a few stress-busting exercises into your routine—relaxation techniques such as meditation, for example, will enable you to switch off from your everyday life. It's also vital that you leave time in your schedule for regular breaks in order to recharge your batteries.

How Healthy Is Your Life?

Research has proved that a healthy mind and body, working together at their peak, will greatly enhance an individual's performance. Yet many people still pay little attention to their health.

But how can being healthy help you to be more successful? Being physically fit gives you the energy and stamina to cope with the stresses of everyday life. When you are in good physical condition, your mind is more alert, your concentration is stronger, and your imagination is freer. You are more likely to have the determination to take the right steps toward achieving your goals and being successful.

On these two pages there are some questions to help you assess how healthy your lifestyle is. Answer Yes or No to each, then turn to "Solutions," on page 139, for an analysis of the answers.

Alcohol and smoking

Today, despite all the medical information and health campaigns, the use of both alcohol and smoking remains remarkably high. They diminish performance and when used over long periods of time can cause life-threatening illnesses, such as

Physical Fitness

- Do you perform an aerobic exercise for at least 20 minutes, three times a week?
- Do you allow your body plenty of rest time in between exercise periods?
- For health benefits, do you tend to enjoy aerobic exercises, such as running, swimming, or walking, rather than more cosmetic or anaerobic exercises, like weight training or yoga?
- Do you make a point of using the stairs even when there is an elevator available?
- Do you choose to walk to work or to the shops instead of taking public transportation or driving?
- If you are under the age of 50, can you do at least 20 sit-ups in 60 seconds?
- Do you have a healthy pulse rate (a healthy pulse rate is below 72 beats per minute at rest for men under the age of 40; below 80 beats per minute at rest for women under the age of 40)?

Daily Diet

- When cooking, do you use polyunsaturated and monosaturated oils, such as sunflower and olive oil?
- On an average day, do you drink less than three beverages containing high levels of caffeine, including coffee, tea, and colas?
- Do you make a point of eating six or more tablespoons of pulses, such as beans and lentils, and whole grains like brown rice each day?
- Do you drink milk that is skimmed or semi-skimmed instead of full-fat?
- Do you always check food packaging for the expiry date or the freshness of the food before you start to prepare a meal?
- Do you try to eat processed and convenience foods as little as possible?
- When you eat breakfast cereal, do you make a conscious effort to have a high-fiber variety in preference to one that is sugar-coated?
- When you feel hungry and want to have a snack in between meals, do you eat raw vegetables or fruit instead of potato chips or cookies?
- Do you trim away all the visible fat from meat before you cook it?
- When you purchase canned fish, do you choose the type that is packed in water rather than oil?
- Do you make a conscious effort to eat foods that help you to keep your body weight under control and maintain a healthy lifestyle?

• Do you warm up for at least ten minutes each time before you do any strenuous exercise?
• When you exercise, do you start out slowly and build gradually to your top performance rate?
• Does your sportswear fit comfortably?

heart disease and cancer. Cutting down on alcohol and quitting smoking must be high priorities for anyone who wants to improve his or her health.

Alcohol when handled in moderation needn't be avoided. The maximum safe limits for consuming alcohol are 21 units for men and 14 for women per week. A unit is equivalent to half a pint of beer, one glass of wine, or a single measure of spirits. As far as smoking is concerned, there is no safe limit. If you are serious about maintaining good health, then you must not smoke.

Relaxation techniques

Learning how to relax is essential for good health and when it is practiced regularly it has a wide variety of benefits including reducing stress levels. It also provides you with the more obvious benefit of allowing you to "switch off" when you feel yourself becoming tense. This enables you to function more effectively in all aspects of your life. Some common relaxation techniques are meditation, yoga, and aromatherapy. See "Raise Your Energy Levels," on page 120, for a more detailed explanation of these ways to relax.

Stress and Relaxation

• Do you know how to recognize the signs of stress?
• Do you take regular breaks during the day in order to wind down and compose yourself?
• Do you plan each day's events so that you are more in control of your time?
• Do you routinely perform some type of relaxation technique, such as meditation or yoga?
• Do you get plenty of sleep?
• At home, are you able to switch off from stress at work?
• Do you spend time talking to your partner or close friends about the problems in your life?
• Do you exercise or find other physical activities to help you relieve stress instead of drinking alcohol or taking tranquillizers?
• Do you know about other techniques—such as massage and aromatherapy—which can aid relaxation?
• Do you make regular visits to your doctor, and are you aware exactly what "good health" means?

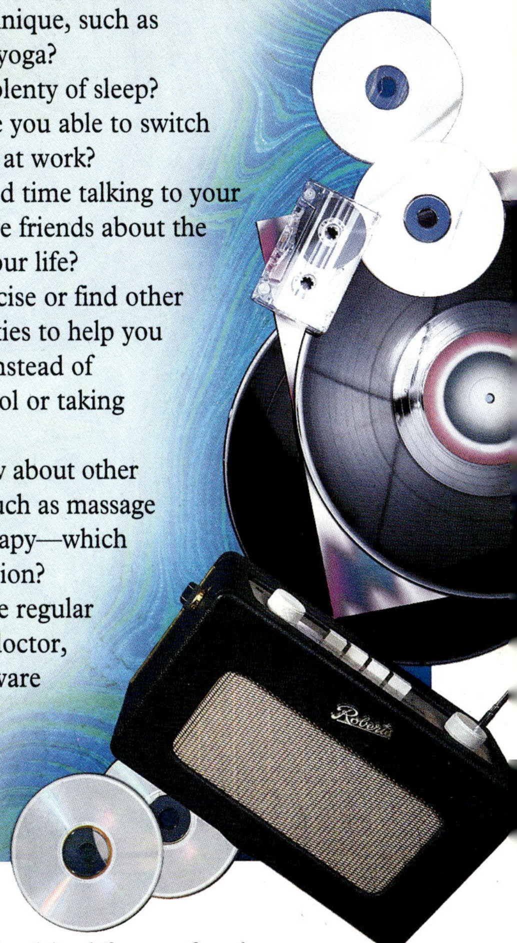

To start living a healthy life you first have to place your health above all else. This attitude change is essential. Too many people spend their lives taking their mental and physical health for granted. They assume that ill-health won't happen to them, or that their doctor will be able to cure whatever ails them. This is a potentially harmful attitude. The only person who can take responsibility for your health is *you*. After all, prevention is always better than cure, and many illnesses or states of ill-health cannot be cured instantly or simply. It is far better to ensure that you are in good health in the first place.

Academic Success

AN IMPRESSIVE ACADEMIC record is commonly perceived as necessary for a successful life. But academic success is like success of any other kind: before you aim for it, or worry that you don't have it, you first have to ask what it means to you. Is it about striving to achieve a particular goal—a degree, perhaps, or a job? Or do you have a genuine love of learning, or a deep passion for a particular subject?

As children, we are eager to explore the world, and curious about everything in it. What happens to this natural curiosity? Perhaps the biggest difference between an adult and a child struggling to learn is that a young child isn't usually afraid of making mistakes, and doesn't know what it means to fail. By the time he or she reaches school age, however, this curiosity is affected by a new understanding of the concept of success and failure; an older sister teases her brother when he falls down, or a teacher gets annoyed when a child misspells a word. In short, we learn that when we do something right, we are admired and approved of; when we get it wrong, we are scolded and sometimes humiliated.

Thus, the sheer pleasure of learning is tempered by internal and external pressure to get things right, to succeed—a pressure that increases steadily as we go through school and on to university.

A love of learning

When psychologists studied people who absorbed information easily and excelled in exams, they found that the high achievers shared two characteristics, instilled in them as children: a love of learning and an active curiosity about the world. You can help your children to develop these invaluable qualities by encouraging them to explore, to ask questions, and to act independently. Avoid putting pressure on them to succeed, and try not to choose their interests for them in an unconscious attempt to fulfill your own frustrated ambitions. Remember that while competition is a necessary element in all learning and achievement, winning, when it is an end in itself, can be very destructive. Children—and adults—who feel free to make choices for themselves, and follow their own instincts, have a far better chance of achieving success than those who feel pressurized into doing something they don't want to do.

It's never too late

People who don't do well at school often feel that they are inadequate when it comes to their past academic record; this insecurity can then hold them back from further career or personal achievement. It's never too late, however, to learn new subjects or skills—or simply to enjoy the learning process. If you would like to return to studying—to further your career, or merely for intellectual stimulation—you may wonder if you will cope in such an alien environment. These fears, however, often have their roots more in unhappy memories of school than in present-day reality. If you are unsure whether a particular course is suitable, enquire about any tests that will help you assess your natural aptitudes and guide you toward appropriate areas of study.

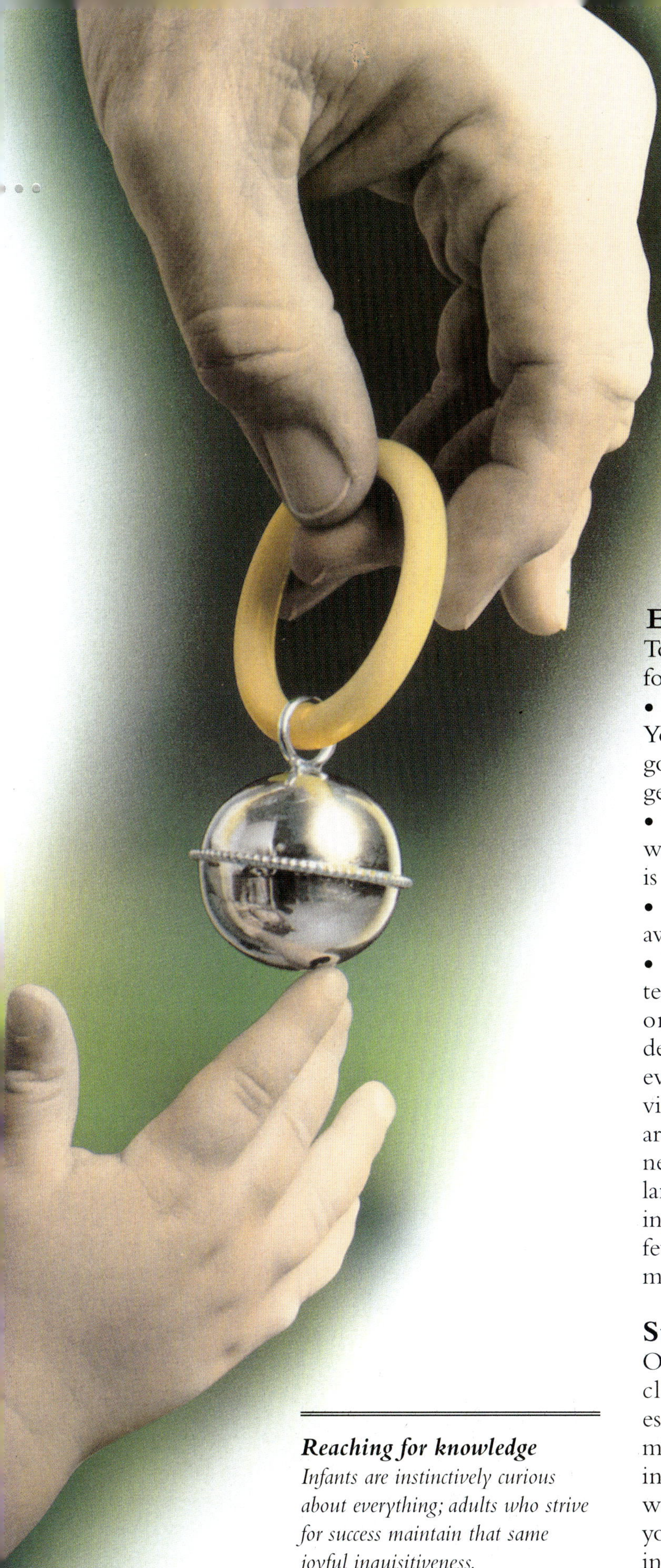

Reaching for knowledge
Infants are instinctively curious about everything; adults who strive for success maintain that same joyful inquisitiveness.

Effective learning

To help you get the most from your studies, the following guidelines might be helpful:

- Make a note of your strengths and weaknesses. You may, for example, work quickly or have a good memory. When you list any weaknesses, don't get carried away and damage your self-esteem.
- Take criticism without hurt or resentment, and welcome it from those you respect. In most cases, it is meant to help, not discourage you.
- Make a list of your problem areas based on self-awareness as well as sound criticism from others.
- Focus on each weakness separately, and using the technique of deconstruction—breaking it down in order to understand its various causes—try to devise ways of overcoming it. Remember that not every weakness requires detailed analysis before a viable solution presents itself. For example, if you are struggling with Italian pronunciation, you may need to listen to the language being spoken regularly, and investing in a set of audio cassettes, listening to an Italian radio station if possible, or hiring a few Italian movies on video could make an enormous difference to your fluency.

Surefire success

Other weaknesses, such as poor performance in class, may be due more to your own low self-esteem than to any lack of intellectual ability, and may therefore require professional help or counseling. The most important thing is to get to grips with your problem areas as early as possible so that you can spend all of your energy positively, learning the most that you can, and enjoying the education process for its own sake.

Develop a Super Memory

Whether you just want to remember the names of new people you meet, or retain the information necessary to pass exams, a good memory is a valuable asset, and one worth developing if you want to be successful. Although you might think that some people are able to recall facts easily, in reality their remarkable memory is often a result of using specific techniques, rather than a product of natural ability.

Understand your memory

According to psychologists, your memory is comprised of three interacting parts—sensory, short-term, and long-term—and these transmit messages back and forth, processing and deciphering the information they receive. The most transient of the three is sensory memory, which stores sights, sounds, and smells and lasts a fleeting four seconds at most.

Next comes short-term memory, the system that holds something in your mind—a telephone number, say—for as long as it takes you to dial—about 30 seconds. Anything you remember for longer than that has been passed from your short-term memory to the third type, long-term memory. Most memory lapses, from failing to remember a colleague's name to forgetting the capital of Italy, result not from losing information, but from an inability to retrieve it from long-term memory.

Short-term memory makes sense of the input the brain receives from the outside world. It acts like a sieve, sorting out what will be preserved and what will fall immediately into oblivion—like the faces of the people on a bus journey, for example. Any effort you put into remembering the information that enters your short-term memory—repeating a

poem until you know it by heart, for instance—ensures that it is passed on to your long-term memory for much more permanent storage.

Mind games

As we get older, our memory tends to become less efficient, and this process can begin as early as the mid or late thirties. The reasons for this are complex and not completely understood, but they are likely to involve a combination of inevitable degeneration, and the fact that, as time passes, our storehouse of memories becomes greater, making individual facts more difficult to find.

Some psychologists believe that we lose our ability to remember as we grow older because we stop landmarking—that is to say, the habit of linking special events to information. The things you will remember more easily are those that are linked to special emotions or events, for example what the weather was like on the day you got your first job. Because as we grow older we experience increasingly fewer such landmark events, we are less likely to remember new information.

Feed your memory

Using unusual visual techniques is an effective way of linking familiar and new facts, such as a PIN number, so that the new facts are more easily remembered.

Scientists have discovered, however, that people who keep their intellect healthy by exercising it and continuing to learn new things are much more likely to remain alert.

Linking information

There is a wide range of techniques you can employ to keep your memory—and your mind—fit and functioning at any age. One of the most effective is linking what you want to remember with other significant information. Scientists and researchers have proved that people remember new facts best when they are connected with as many as possible of the following:

- sensory experiences
- strong emotions
- important associations
- necessity for survival
- personal meaning
- repetition
- anything unique or different
- beginnings and endings

You can use this knowledge to increase the ways you help yourself to remember. For instance, the code for your new PIN number is 1330, and you are worried you will not remember it. But you know that 1330, or 1.30pm, is lunchtime, so imagine food laid out in those numbers, as though you were going to eat them. You can also make the association between your PIN number and feeling hungry, or you could imagine your lunch being dispensed by a cash machine. The most important thing is that the more unusual links you can make, the more chances you have to remember.

Unusual connections

There are other ways, too, of remembering the figures 1330. For instance, if you are aged 30 now, get an image of yourself age 13, anchoring it to something specific which happened to you at that age. Then you could picture yourself as both people, jostling each other as they try to get money from the cash machine. To find the methods that work best for you, you may have to use a process of trial and error. The result will repay your efforts, though, since having a good memory can help you in many aspects of your life—therefore it is up to you to keep your memory in good working order.

Memory Tips

Perhaps the best-known memory technique is a visual one; make a knot—in your tie, for example, or in a string around your finger—as a reminder to do something, like make a phone call. Below are a few alternative memory tactics:

• **Association.** The next time you meet someone new, try the following:
1. Repeat his or her name to yourself several times, out loud if possible.
2. If you know others by the same name, picture them all together.
3. Then picture the person you have just met doing something different.
4. Find a physical feature that stands out.
5. Link the name to something relevant.

For example, you are introduced to Jane at a conference. You know at least five other Janes, so this could be tricky. Begin by repeating her name: "Hello, Jane." You might add a word about her job in order provide a memory "hook." "I've been hearing a lot about the marketing department," for example.

Next, visualize this Jane sitting with all your other Janes, then imagine her standing, to set her apart from the others. If she has a distinguishing feature such as a gap in her teeth, use this, by association, to remember her name. For example, Jane is in marketing and fills the gaps in the market.

• **Word rhymes**, tricks, slogans, and acronyms can be very helpful. Advertisers know this very well—think of all the catchy jingles that stick in your mind, even after the product is no longer available. Likewise, most adults remember the spelling rhymes they learned at school—however long ago.

• **Repetition.** Saying or writing something over and over again can be useful for getting facts into your head. Likewise, jotting things down or listing everything you have to do are both simple, but extremely effective, memory aids.

Creative Success

Creativity comes in many different forms. We tend to associate it most strongly, of course, with artists, such as painters, composers, writers, and so on. But the scientific leap of imagination that led to discovering penicillin in a dish of mold is also a type of creativity, albeit a very different one. While you may never achieve the graphic brilliance of Rembrandt, compose music on a par with Mozart, or equal the scientific insight of Stephen Hawking, whenever you try something different, or approach a problem in a new way, you are being creative. Even mundane domestic responsibilities, when approached in a fresh, original way, can offer enormous scope for creativity. For example, when you entertain a bored toddler by improvising a toy out of cardboard packaging, or brighten up an otherwise ordinary meal by arranging a handful of twigs and grasses in an old coffee mug for the table centerpiece, you are being creative. Making an effort to harness and cultivate this creativity at every opportunity can enrich every area of your life.

The creativity myth

We don't know precisely how the creative process works, or why it comes more easily to some people than to others. What we do know, however, is that many assumptions about the nature of creative genius are deeply flawed. One of the most common, for example, is the existence of the "flash of inspiration"—the sudden arrival, as if by magic, of the concept for a brilliant piece of music, a great painting, or a revolutionary scientific discovery.

In fact, the foundation of all creativity is constructed from knowledge, experience, and endless effort. Inspirational flashes virtually always come at the end of a long period of hard work, sometimes stretching over years of study and contemplation. The painter Pablo Picasso, for example, devoted a huge amount of time and energy learning about art history and mastering the techniques of composition and drawing before he began to explore the radical abstract style for which he became famous. Similarly, the structure of DNA did not suddenly come to John Watson and Francis Crick with the simplicity of a light bulb being switched on. It was the result of thousands of hours of painstaking, often frustrating, research by many highly trained and dedicated scientists.

The tortured genius

Another false notion is that truly creative personalities are, by definition, deeply unhappy, if not eccentric, alcoholic, or even insane: the heartbroken clown and the mad inventor are two common manifestations of this stereotype. Although some people do turn to artistic expression, or immersion in work of any kind, as a way of coming to terms with—or avoiding—crises, there is no direct link between emotional

A work of art
Building creativity into all aspects of your life will improve even the most mundane things you have to do.

distress or other psychiatric malfunction and the creative process. On the contrary, mental illness of any kind, even mild depression or anxiety, has an adverse effect on creativity. In order to be creative—to originate ideas and to have the confidence to carry them through—you do have to be functioning reasonably well, both physically and emotionally.

Common qualities

There are a number of characteristics that tend to be shared by creative personalities:

- They live fully in the moment, focused on their immediate surroundings and the task at hand. At its most extreme, this quality can result in selfishness and lack of consideration for others.
- They are not restricted unnecessarily by stereotypes, conventions, or other people's values, beliefs, and expectations. This trait is responsible, in part, for the clichéd image of the artist or scientist as an odd, wild, or eccentric figure.
- They are often spontaneous, expressive, and unpredictable, with an appropriate lack of inhibition. This is not the same as a total absence of control and discipline, however, which is always destructive.
- They are comparatively tolerant and relaxed in their attitudes toward life.
- Whatever their age, they have many childlike qualities, such as the ability to enjoy playing spontaneously and unselfconsciously, and are trusting and innocent.
- They will take risks and are not afraid of making mistakes or looking foolish.
- They are not handicapped by fear of the unknown, the mysterious, or the puzzling.
- They put a great deal of trust in their instincts, relying on their own feelings to tell them what's right.

Reap the rewards

Many people consider creativity notable only when it produces a tangible end result—a work of art or an important discovery—instead of seeing it as an enlightened way of living. Many brilliant and successful creative figures, however, often lead less-than-successful lives because they put so much energy and imagination into their work that they have nothing left for their family and friends—or for themselves.

So, while you may think of yourself as not having a creative job, remember that you have the potential to be creative in all aspects of your life.

Learn to Live Creatively

Although you may think you're not very creative, in fact your everyday life is filled with creative ideas, thoughts, and ways of doing things. Everyone has the capacity to be creative, and there are concrete steps you can take to enable yourself to think creatively. You've probably looked through a kaleidoscope, and know that when you turn the end, the glass pieces rearrange themselves into different patterns. In the same way, we can use different methods of thinking to create new solutions.

Creative thinking

Creativity doesn't come in a flash. It has to be worked at. Some solutions seem to arrive at ordinary moments—the inspirational idea that occurs while you're putting out the trash, for example. But what has in fact happened is that all the thinking you've been doing has come together on an unconscious level. This is why, paradoxically, the more you try, the less likely you are to reach a solution.

All creative thinking is built upon a foundation of knowledge. So, if you are faced with some new situation—not necessarily a problem, but something at which you want to do your best—you need to find out as much as you can about every aspect of it. For example, if you were thinking of adding a conservatory to your house, you would first have to investigate the local zoning regulations, the site, the potential cost, and which company supplied the best builders. Then you would consult design magazines and books, look at other people's conservatories, think about colors, and so on.

At this point, you would enter the do-nothing phase, a vital stage in all creative thinking. By doing nothing, you are letting your mind digest, then integrate all the knowledge you have taken in. Not forcing yourself to act immediately will allow your creative thinking to flow. Sometimes doing physical work—gardening, mowing the lawn, washing the car—is a good way of allowing your unconscious to get to work. At some point ideas will start to filter through, which you might want to write down. Then, you will be able to use your critical skills to accept or reject them.

Finding strategies

Thinking creatively usually involves several modes of thought, in different combinations and at different stages. These include critical, analytical, and strategic thinking. Critical thinking involves evaluating something carefully, and weighing up the pros and cons in detail. For example, if you want to buy a house, you consider all the options, looking at which serves your needs best.

A different angle

Looking at life in unusual ways, and trying new things, can enrich your life in ways you had not predicted.

Add color to your day
Bringing creativity to the way you live, to every moment of your day, even in small ways, will brighten your life.

Analytical thinking starts with breaking a problem into parts, analyzing each one, and then thinking about how to put the parts together in a different way. Advertisers, for instance, have to think analytically to create new ways of selling an existing product. Strategic thinking is a form of step-by-step analysis which looks at planning on a large scale, such as building a bridge, and involves juggling many priorities.

Outcome thinking

One way to approach problems is to look first at what the solution, or outcome, might be. Outcome thinking means focusing on the result. This can be a great help, particularly if you are trying to get to grips with a personal problem.

Consider yourself five years in the future. You are satisfied with your life. Imagine that a journalist is coming to interview you. Try to imagine what the story would say, or even write it down. Let your mind and imagination go—you may be surprised at what you find out. For instance, you may fantasize about being a public servant, able to convey your opinions to others. So you decide that you want to enter politics, and you may want to research how other people have achieved this so that you can learn from them. Alternatively, consider what you would like to be said about you at your memorial service: what would you like to have achieved, what experiences would you like to have had, and what sort of person would you like to be? By starting at the end point in this way, you can learn what steps you need to take now.

Learning creativity

Being creative shouldn't be stressful: the key word is play. Ironically, it's by enjoying yourself that you will become more creative. If you can let your mind play with different ideas, moving them around and putting them together in new shapes and images, you will be able to generate fresh ideas.

Once you get the knack of this kind of thinking you will find it immensely helpful. You don't need to change your life radically, just make slow, small changes, risking things that you might have dismissed in the past. Examples of these tactics might include:

- taking a different route to work
- taking a trip to a place you've never been before
- doing something physically challenging
- reading different kinds of books and magazines
- trying to meet people who aren't in your usual crowd or profession

The idea is to start looking at things in a different way. If what you're doing does not work, try something else. Don't take it too seriously, or have a concrete set of goals—just have fun.

FAMILY SUCCESS

MANY OF US are brought up to believe that a successful family is always happy, harmonious, and well-behaved. As an exercise, what do you think of the following dialogue?

Sam: It's Daddy! Daddy's home! Hi, Daddy!
Dad: Hi, son. How was school today?
Sam: Not so good, Dad. I failed another math test.
Dad: Don't worry, son, you can't be good at everything. Let's get together this evening and have a look at what you're having problems with. Hello, darling [to wife].

Mom: Hello, sweetheart. How was the office?
Dad: Terrible, but I'll survive. I got these for you [handing her some flowers].
Mom: Oh, darling, you remembered our anniversary! I've made a special meal, too.

However unrealistic you may think this seems, it isn't actually that far off from what many of us are brought up to feel we should aim for where family life is concerned. And despite all the evidence that the nature of the family in the twentieth century is changing dramatically, the media often persist in presenting family images that have little to do with modern reality. When our own families don't measure up to these images, we feel somehow that we've failed, but we're not sure how, or what to do about it. So how can we aim for family success?

Where do you fit in?

Psychologists will tell you that, in any group, and especially in families, it's inevitable that each person will take on—or be given—a particular role. Role-playing isn't necessarily unhealthy, as long as the individual concerned doesn't feel trapped by it. Working out what family role you play will help you to see where you fit in the scheme of things, and whether you are still repeating good or bad habits.

For example, thanks to a period of counseling, Peter has recently been able to identify his family role. Soon after his father died, Peter, the eldest child, grew up very quickly, and became responsible for taking care of his mother. As an adult, family life does not "agree" with him, and he has been divorced twice. As soon as he gets within a family unit, he starts to feel he has to give up too much personal freedom—a freedom he feels he was cheated of when younger. This has also left him with feelings of resentment toward his mother which have soured relations between them. Now that he has a better understanding of what his role was, Peter is able to learn to shed the burden of his unwanted role and feel more comfortable and honest in his relationships.

Sarah is a very different case. Her parents always treated her as an equal from an early age, and she developed a healthy sense of responsibility that made her the "organized" one in the family. As an adult, she thrives on being able to deal with whatever life throws at her.

The roles family members adopt are often taken without conscious thought, and children tend to mold their behavior to fit in with their parents' needs, no matter how damaging that might be. Try to initiate discussion as to what roles you and other family members play.

Express yourself

The ability to express emotions is very important when it comes to understanding families and so making them work better. It's impossible—and unhealthy—for people to live together without any conflict. Yet many people seem to think that families shouldn't show feelings, such as anger, and the message "keep it to yourself" gets passed on.

Life will become less rocky if you acknowledge that the family is a reservoir of potent feelings that extend far into the past. Problems and emotions that haven't been resolved in the past will often surface in the present—for example, a daughter might remind her mother of a sister she envied.

Like father, like son

Even when it's not in their interests, children usually follow their parents' example.

Your feelings—or theirs?

For many of us, the process of taking on generations of family beliefs and habits is unconscious—we simply act in a certain way. Yet every so often you may experience a moment when you think to yourself, "That's just what my father used to say." Despite your attempts to be different, you may have taken on your parents' views and feelings, and are perhaps passing them on to your own children.

Don't automatically condemn any identification with your parents. This is a part of normal, healthy development and it's how, for better as well as for worse, you learned to be an adult. Make a list of the various ways in which you feel you echo your parents' values and behavior. For example, if your parents never allowed the open expression of anger, and you always tell your own children to be quiet when they get angry, you might need to think about who is saying this, and why.

Tipped for success

Once you appreciate these inherited or emulated patterns, you can build better relationships based on greater understanding of family dynamics. Start by being aware of your family's healthy and unhealthy aspects, and encourage open discussion if you can—sweeping issues under the carpet only stores up problems for the future. Also, don't assume that change equals disruption—the family is a living organism that changes from one minute to the next. Again, discussion is the key—you need to understand why family members are changing, or you may just feel that the family is falling apart for no reason or that they are changing to spite you.

Make sure that each family member is allowed to be themselves and to express their feelings openly. Look for the continuation of negative family characteristics from the past. It will help if you base your behavior in reality, and make it clear to the family that you feel that mistakes and conflicts are allowed—and don't have to be neatly resolved.

How to Make Your Family Work

In fairytales, happy families are remarkable for the total harmony in which they live, every member exuding optimism, cheerfulness, and unflinching courage in the face of adversity. In real life, however, successful families—that is, those that produce emotionally fulfilled individuals—recognize that such idealized images are completely unrealistic.

Families that function in a healthy way also have a number of specific characteristics in common.

A flexible family

Truly successful families will be able to contain positive and negative emotions and know that family love will survive.

Such families enjoy open, honest communication, personal differences are valued, the privacy of each member is respected, individuals are listened to, and appropriate boundaries are well established.

The importance of communication

Expressing your feelings—especially negative ones—in an honest way is seldom easy, particularly with those who are closest to you, and with whom you are most vulnerable. Accepting and expressing these feelings, far from leading to chaos and family breakdown, is, however, absolutely essential. This is because stifled emotions don't disappear; they either simmer away until they become bitter and violent, or they turn inward and produce depression and anxiety. Secure, emotionally healthy people with a strong sense of self-worth understand that family love will survive the negative emotions—such as envy, jealousy, or greed—that everybody experiences.

Valuing differences

Many people find it disturbing when their close relations—particularly children—differ markedly from the family, whatever form that difference takes. For example, a family whose members excel in sports may not be able to cope with a son or daughter who has no interest in that direction. Similarly, a traditional family with no experience of homosexuality can have difficulty accepting a gay son or daughter. Too often, parents' misplaced feelings of guilt, embarrassment and prejudice blot out more important concerns about their child's emotional happiness.

It's vital for everyone in a family to accept that their loved ones are unique and that their individuality should be celebrated rather than stifled. Setbacks encountered in the exploration of individuality should be met with compassion rather than served up as proof that the conventional path should have been followed.

The need for space

A family in which there is no space for anyone to be private is a breeding ground for tension and discontent. In this regard, physical space is less important than emotional space—acceptance of each person's right to his or her own emotions and thoughts. So, while it's normal for parents to enquire about their children's whereabouts, constant demands for every detail of the company they keep, the relationships they form, and their innermost feelings are overpowering and unreasonable.

Parents should maintain a degree of privacy from their children, both for the health of their own relationship, and for the children's sake. While children need to feel loved, they also need parents who are whole, separate people. Those who sacrifice their lives to their offspring impose a burden, for no child should feel responsible for a parent's happiness.

Listening and hearing

We all have times when we need the undivided attention of someone close. In families where there is not enough attention to go round, a child's craving for it may manifest itself in behavioral problems. What's more, when partners fail to listen to each other, not only does their relationship suffer, but the resulting unhappiness makes them less able to listen to their children, so perpetuating the vicious circle.

To feel safe, children need discipline. If they think that their parents aren't strong enough to set boundaries, they sense that they, not their parents, are in control. Their constant testing of boundaries—in the form of antisocial behavior—is often, particularly in adolescence, a way of expressing a profound need to feel secure and loved at a time of enormous hormonal and emotional change in their lives.

Wise parents remain flexible and are able to compromise when it's appropriate. Whereas weak boundaries cannot hold the family together, those that are too rigid can crack: You would be ill-advised, for example, to give in out of sheer exhaustion to a child's pleas to be allowed out all night. On the other hand, there is nothing to be gained from dogged adherence to such a ruling in light of changed circumstances, simply because you would interpret a change of heart as an erosion of your authority.

Individual guidelines

While all these guidelines can be of considerable value in creating an effective, harmonious family unit, it's important that you interpret and adjust them to suit each individual personality and circumstance that crops up in the web of family life.

Pushing back the barriers

Children are always trying to expand the boundaries that curtail what they can do.

SUCCESS IN LOVE

"WHAT IS THIS THING called love?" Cole Porter's lyrics aptly sum up the mystery of an emotion that has puzzled and fascinated humankind ever since we first started being aware of emotions. More than any other topic, love and relationships are what we spend most of our time thinking and dreaming about, and agonizing over.

It is difficult, if not impossible, to define or measure "success in love," for a happy relationship means different things to different people (see "A Fine Romance," pp. 66-67). However, there are common problems that will threaten any relationship, no matter how you choose to shape it. Perhaps the major cause of breakdown is that after the initial excitement of being "in love," people lose sight of the fact that a successful relationship must be worked at continuously. Love will not succeed by itself: you must care about it, and be very positive and determined to make it work.

Working at love

The first step in working at your relationship is to analyze your feelings, to know who you are, and be sure of your own expectations of relationships in general, before you get to grips with those of someone else. In the case of Karen and Dick this important exercise was always ignored. They had an exciting, secret, whirlwind romance at work and within a year they were married. Once the honeymoon period was over, however, the differences in their characters became apparent. Dick was mostly a stay-at-home type, whereas Karen loved to go out socializing with friends. By failing to confront this fundamental difference or, more importantly, the frustration it was causing both parties, they simply ended up doing their own thing and resenting how the other person spent his or her spare time.

After ten years of marriage, Dick declared that he wanted a divorce, and that he had met someone else. Karen claimed that she was totally shocked by Dick's unhappiness, although deep down she had suspected that he had been frustrated and discontent for some time. Of course there were many complex reasons for the breakdown of the relationship—such as the couple's failure to communicate and their very different personalities—but it is possible that they could have made it work or ended it sooner if they had taken the time to nurture their relationship and discuss their true feelings.

A flexible friendship

In every type of relationship, there will be difficult times. To be able to cope positively with crises, both partners—in addition to being honest, sensitive, and patient—need to strive to be flexible and remain willing and open to compromise. But problems and setbacks do not always threaten relationships, and may even strengthen them, often by helping the couple to realize how

EARLY LOVE

What kind of relationship did your parents have? We learn what is acceptable behavior through identification with our parents. If they expressed warm and loving feelings, then we too will feel it's acceptable to have and share such feelings.

Early separation and loss, unless successfully mourned, can lead to a negative attitude toward close relationships. The person will always expect the worst—abandonment—and may even bring about separation to speed up what is perceived to be inevitable.

Do you feel you got enough of your parents' love? Sometimes parents fail to appreciate the depth of their children's needs. If you feel you never got enough love, you may be demanding more from your current partner than he or she is able to give.

Did you feel that you and your siblings were rivals for your parents' love and attention? In adult life, this may manifest itself in feeling envious of our peers, or even our partner or own children, and in needing constant attention and reassurance that we are loved.

much they really mean to each other. This was so with Bernard and Jane.

As the youngest child and only son, Bernard had always been very close to his mother, and his mother very dependent on him. Even after he got married to Jane, Bernard visited his frail, housebound mother several days a week, and nearly every Sunday. This was becoming a problem for Jane, who was particularly worried about how things would work when their first child was born in a few months time. She had never really discussed her feelings with Bernard because she felt that his loyalty to his mother was an admirable quality and that she was probably being unreasonable. She had decided just to wait and see what happened when the baby arrived; but before the baby was born Bernard's mother fell down some stairs. Although her injuries were slight it was a difficult time. Jane was very supportive of Bernard, but she also voiced her own anxieties about their future. Bernard was surprised to learn of her feelings, but they both found great strength in their ability to talk about their problems, although there was no easy solution. They managed to set up satisfactory arrangements for his mother's care and their relationship not only survived the crisis, but was stronger as a result.

Learning about love

If a relationship does not succeed you should not feel despondent or fear that you are a failure—a breakdown is rarely the fault of only one person and may be due to forces beyond your control.

Although each relationship is unique, you should always try to learn from your past experiences, draw some positive conclusions from them, and be honest about your own part—in the successes and the failures. It may only be after several serious relationships that you discover what it is you need and want from another person—and from yourself.

A Fine Romance

Despite our experiences to the contrary, most of us continue to hope for, and believe in, a storybook romance that will last happily ever after. We think the person we choose to love will fulfill our every need and wish, understand us perfectly, and support us through thick and thin. Then, when we begin to see that our knight in shining armor has dents and rusty spots, or our beautiful princess has a few stray hairs, we are apt to feel angry and cheated. Whether we can learn to adapt and accept the real person will depend on whether we are willing to accept reality, or need to keep on living a romantic fantasy.

Taking the knocks
Minor faults, like clumsiness, don't affect healthy relationships.

Mr. Fat and Mrs. Lean

You will almost certainly have met couples who left you wondering how two such different people manage to live together in apparent love and harmony. What is it that makes two people compatible, despite very obvious differences between them?

If you have been involved in a close, long-term relationship you will be aware that, at some point, you begin to think of, and view, your partner as an extension of yourself. This is because couples often act as two halves of a whole—what you can't see in one person is often expressed by the other. For example, where one partner is painfully shy and introverted, the other may be outgoing and sociable, or where one person is the "brains" and the other is the "brawn."

More than skin deep
You don't have to try to look your best all the time in order to be loved.

True love—what is it?

Once you have found your "other half," whether the relationship survives or not is the result of many complex factors. The most important factor, however, will be what you personally mean by "love." Real love is wanting to be with a person because they are who they are. If you feel you must make someone into Prince Charming or Miss Perfect, and can't tolerate any signs that they are really mere mortals, you won't be able to cope with the frustrations of everyday life. Loving another person is loving all of them, including their faults, their weakness, and their problems. This doesn't mean you necessarily *like* everything about them, but that you accept that. In the case of Ralph and John, the point of contention lies in the way Ralph always

leaves the kitchen after preparing a meal. He believes the mess and the washing up can wait. John explodes and rants—but both of them know this doesn't affect John's basic feelings for Ralph. Being angry doesn't mean not loving.

Domestic detail
Messiness is irritating, but it won't erode love.

Freedom is also part of real love. Each person needs to feel secure enough in their love and in the relationship to allow the other to explore, grow, and change. For some people, this means living in a way that isn't considered "normal" by others. Sarah and Roger, for example, decided early in their relationship that neither of them wanted to give up their successful jobs in their respective cities in order to live together—they had tried it and it didn't work. So, much to the horror of their friends, they got married and then proceeded to live four hundred miles apart, meeting up on weekends. Their marriage is still going strong, while many of their friends' more conventional marriages have failed.

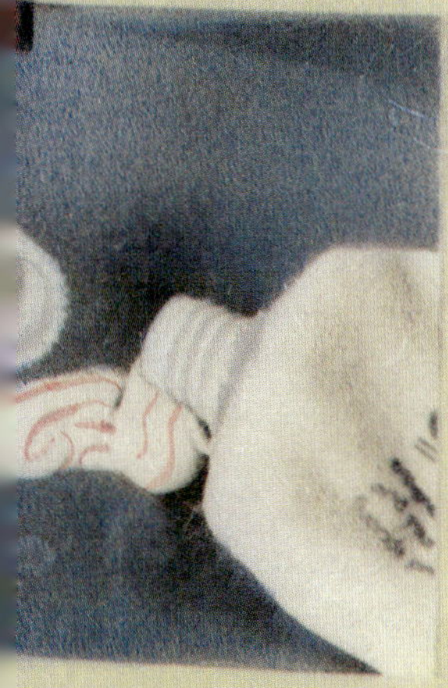

It's the little things
Your personal habits can drive partners to distraction without driving them away.

Trust and acceptance

Real love allows all kinds of feelings to be expressed freely and openly. There is a mutual trust that, despite your faults, you will be loved as a person, as a whole. Tracy and Tom had a very tempestuous relationship, involving loud arguments that ended in one of them storming out of the house. But the relationship lasted many years because Tracy and Tom were able to express their love as freely as their anger. No argument was so serious that it was not followed soon afterwards by an intense and passionate period of "making-up."

The real world
Happy couples love each other as they are.

Finally, to love another person, you must love and accept yourself. If you are highly self-critical, you will be the same with your partner. If you feel at heart you are a "bad" and unlovable person, you will never be able to accept another's love—nor will you be able to accept and love them. No amount of love from another person will make up for a lack of self-worth—to love, you must feel you can be truly loved yourself, warts and all!

SOCIAL SUCCESS

A NETWORK OF CLOSE FRIENDS and like-minded acquaintances is one of the keys of happiness. Having a successful social life, however, is not a matter of fraternizing with hundreds of people. Social success is principally about spending rewarding time with people you like and respect, who like and respect you in return.

When your confidence is at a low ebb, it's easy to believe that everyone except you is constantly out in an endless whirl of dinners, dances, and parties. You may even fear there is something wrong with you if you spend time on your own.

In fact, most people find social occasions nerve-wracking, and those who cope with them most effectively are aware of this; they don't try too hard, and as a result, they are able to put others at ease. In many cases, the facility for producing a constant stream of witty, inconsequential chatter conceals a profound lack of confidence and a total inability to engage in natural, spontaneous conversation.

Filling the gaps

Those who feel that they are driven to fill every waking moment with engagements are often quite lonely souls who will do anything to avoid being alone—even if it means engaging in activities that they don't particularly enjoy with people whom they never really talk to. This constant diversion offers protection against periods of solitude in which they might have to face their buried anxiety and self-doubt. What's more, people who operate in this way tend to see a blank diary page as proof of their own worthlessness, in their own eyes and in the view of others. At its most extreme, such insecurity can even lead people to get through an unwanted Saturday night spent at home by drawing the drapes and refusing to answer the telephone in case they reveal to others what they perceive to be their lack of popularity.

A hectic social life should never be mistaken for real social success—that is the capacity to form and sustain a wide range of fulfilling relationships. The ability to spend time alone is not the mark of a social misfit, but often denotes mature, emotionally healthy individuals who enjoy their own company as much as that of others.

Quality not quantity

Social relationships play a vital role in everyone's life. The frequency of the contact with friends is not especially relevant in terms of emotional well-being, for it will, by nature, vary from person to person. For instance, there are some people who like to socialize with a large number of friends regularly, while others are content knowing fewer people and seeing them less frequently. What is important for everyone, however, is the quality of these social relationships—the amount of genuine warmth and sympathy that exists between themselves and others.

The honest approach

To create a fulfilling social life, you should begin by letting your own instincts guide you; never fill your days with activities in which you have no interest, or spend time in the company of people with whom you have nothing in common. Accept the fact that you will not be drawn to everyone you meet and, what is perhaps harder to bear, that everyone you meet will not be drawn to you. While making every attempt to be approachable, friendly, and interested in others, resist the temptation to be constantly agreeable in an attempt to find universal affection and approval. This is not only a fruitless labor, it is also counterproductive, since there are few people more irritating than those whose obsessive desire to please renders them devoid of a unique and positive personality.

Success in numbers?
The ability to spend time in solitary contemplation is an important element of social success.

Far from making you feel fulfilled and successful, taking part in social activities that are not rooted in your own personality and interests will tend only to increase your loneliness and isolation. You will be likely to feel empty and alienated if you are just filling up your diary for the sake of avoiding solitude, and this will decrease your sense of self-esteem. Don't be afraid of new experiences and new people, but ensure you make permanent room in your life only for those who give you a real sense of warmth, connection and belonging.

"LYING" or
"FILLING UP"
DEPRESSION
or LOW
RIDGE OF HIGH PRESSURE
SHAPED
DEPRESSION
HIGH
LOW
OIL DILUTION
TEMP
220 160 100

CHAPTER THREE

How to Get There

YOU HAVE SET YOUR SIGHTS on success, now you must act on your ideas. For all sorts of reasons, many people have a block over getting started, but this chapter will help you to formulate a strategy.

The first step is to make a life plan (see pp. 76-79)—after all, how can you work toward something if you don't know exactly what it is? A plan will help you think things through, keep you heading in the right direction, and give you a greater feeling of commitment. Carrying out your plan will not be easy. You will find it hard to break old habits, and you may be beset by inertia and any number of fears but, as you will see, all these can be overcome.

This chapter also covers many general skills that you will need in order to become more effective in many areas of your life, such as decision-making, effective communication, and good organization and presentation. Some of these skills may seem obvious, or simply a matter of common sense, but it is surprising how few of us actually put into practice what we think we know. A selection of exercises and examples throughout this chapter will help you to focus more clearly on what you should be doing. Low self-esteem is often at the root of an inability to see things through, so it is also important to remind yourself regularly of your capabilities.

Increasingly, in today's fast-paced world, people are looking for more efficient ways to juggle their home and work responsibilities (see "Professional Tactics," pp. 86-91). Childcare, for instance, is an issue of growing importance. More women are pursuing careers as well as having families, and, by choice or necessity, men are taking a greater hand in childcare. Changing times bring new problems, but they also bring new solutions. In some professions new technology is making new ways of working feasible. On pages 102-103, you will find strategies for taking advantage of the new wave of telecommunications and computers that will enable you to gain more control of your life instead of being a slave to work.

Apparently insurmountable obstacles—such as prejudice, discrimination, and sexual harassment—may impede your progress and stop your career in its tracks. Solving any of these problems will be hard but there are techniques that can help you deal with them (see pp. 104-107). Whenever you feel you are not making progress, look to your life plan for inspiration, realize how much you have already achieved, and keep going!

SUCCESS IS YOURS FOR THE TAKING. SO DECIDE EXACTLY WHAT YOU WANT TO ACHIEVE, PLAN YOUR STRATEGY, AND THEN—MOST IMPORTANT OF ALL—PUT IT INTO PRACTICE!

Do It Now!

EVERY DAY YOU probably let opportunities pass right through your fingers. If you jotted down the things you would like to do, or the changes you would like to make to your life, you might well draw up quite a long list. But when it came to putting them into practice, an equally lengthy list of reasons why everything should stay just the same would probably spring instantly to mind. Some of your reasons will be perfectly valid, but most of them are the result of the kind of inertia that bogs everyone down at one time or another. The important thing is not to let this rule your life.

In the palm of your hand
Hang on to the possibilities that cross your path—don't let them get away.

Taking drastic measures

Inertia takes different forms with different people. Janet, for example, is someone who comes into her own in a crisis, and she thrives on making occasional major changes. For instance, she recently decided, after years of putting off an exciting vacation, that she would spend a year traveling around the world.

Janet's friends were impressed by her bold decision, and she herself had a wonderful time. Once back home, however, she got caught up in the "I'll do *x* when I've done *y*" trap. She would tell herself that she would join that evening class after she had decorated her apartment, and that she would get on with that after she had finished sorting out old photos. Janet was able to cope with major events, but was less able to get on top of things and make the most of life on a day-to-day basis. Dissatisfaction built up until every so often she had to release her frustration by taking drastic steps, such as her long vacation.

Doing something dramatic feels as though you are taking such a bold action that it will wipe out all those smaller things you haven't been getting on with. But the small things don't go away—you must face them if you want to make the most of your life. Either that, or you will have to decide that some of the small tasks that are bogging you down simply aren't important, and stop wasting energy thinking about them. To spend your time worrying about not getting things done, and still fail to do them, is the worst possible option.

Tackling change

On the other hand, you may be someone whose daily life runs like a well-oiled machine, but who is terrified by any change that may disrupt this. You pride yourself in getting those everyday things done. But is your well-ordered routine a smokescreen for some of the more fundamental changes you would like to make in your life? You feel that you are making progress because you are always so busy, and you certainly make constant improvements to your quality of life, but think about whether you have other goals you want to achieve. Prepare yourself for the fact that they may mean sacrificing some of your daily achievements.

"I'm so lazy..."

Whatever sort of person you are, when you are reminded of things you could be doing, you probably feel guilty about what you think of as laziness. However, guilt won't get you very far. What will is realizing that:

• You don't need to be perfect; you can't possibly get everything done immaculately. Choose your priority tasks, and do those well now, so that you get a sense of satisfaction from a job done promptly and proficiently. Now get the less important tasks out of the way as well as you can with the time available. Having decided which tasks aren't important and which you haven't got time for, cross them off your list—and then don't give them a second thought.

• Chances are you aren't lazy, you simply haven't tried prioritizing things as outlined above. Either that or you aren't doing anything that fires you with enthusiasm. If you spend all your time slumped in front of the television, think about what you do day after day. Everything can't be ideal, but you may be in a position where you aren't doing *anything* you really want to. This is where you can easily get locked into a cycle of inertia and guilt. Decide on your goals and likes and dislikes, and the rest may start to follow.

Building blocks

You may not have thought about the mental blocks that you have built up for yourself over the years but there are three major obstacles that could be holding you firmly in the grip of "I'll get round to that tomorrow." These mental blocks are:

• **Fear of failure—or of success.** You might not start that novel because you fear discovering that you aren't cut out to be a writer after all, or because, if it were published, your family might be shocked!

• **Lack of information.** Perhaps you lack the facts to act decisively. For example, you might have convinced yourself that shortage of funds is stopping you from returning to school, without looking into any of the grants which may be available.

• **Lack of self-confidence.** Perhaps the best tactic here is to start small, but as you mean to go on—starting to take action, and not just thinking about it. Resolve to take some positive action every day, no matter how small: call up that old friend, buy a magazine you always meant to read—and perhaps give yourself a treat for each action you take.

As you progress, however, become aware of when you are taking an action for the sake of it. Decide whether you must act now to seize an opportunity, or whether it might be prudent to put it off until you have more information or have reflected properly. It's a matter of balance, and of not letting either extreme take over your life.

A clear view
Clear plans and high self-esteem will help you to start seeing the road to your goals.

How Dynamic Are You?

Are you the sort of person who gets on and achieves all that you can in your life? Or would you rather stay in bed all day and do nothing but watch television? In other words, are you dynamic or lazy?

Most people would not like to see themselves as slothful, but everyone is prone to sloth from time to time—whether the form it takes is intellectual or physical. The challenge is to get rid of as much of this wasteful trait as possible, so that you increase your chances of achieving all your ambitions.

Give yourself a boost

Most people could probably use a little boost in the level of their dynamic energy. Instead of just sitting and thinking about doing things, therefore, make a start by looking over the following points and acting on those that have the most relevance for you:

• **Accept responsibility.** People who are emotionally satisfied and fulfilled take full responsibility for doing whatever is necessary in order for them to reach their goals. Remember that nobody ever achieved a full, rich life by daydreaming about it and hoping that it would magically come to pass.

It's important, however, to guard against becoming obsessional about having to take immediate action. Whenever possible, try to act decisively (as opposed to dithering), then be prepared to change your tactics if your planned approach suddenly seems inappropriate, especially if you suspect that it may affect other people in some undesirable or destructive way. Your aim is to be firm and positive without being rigid or ruthless.

• **Keep fit.** Action needs energy, so make every effort to keep yourself in good shape, both mentally and physically. Aim for a well-balanced combination of sensible eating, regular exercise, sufficient rest, and appropriate relaxation and leisure activities. Without being too strict with yourself, try to cut down on unhealthy habits such as smoking, drinking, and overeating.

• **Set realistic goals.** Establish a number of goals that really inspire you, and that you will enjoy working toward. Pursuits that you value and take

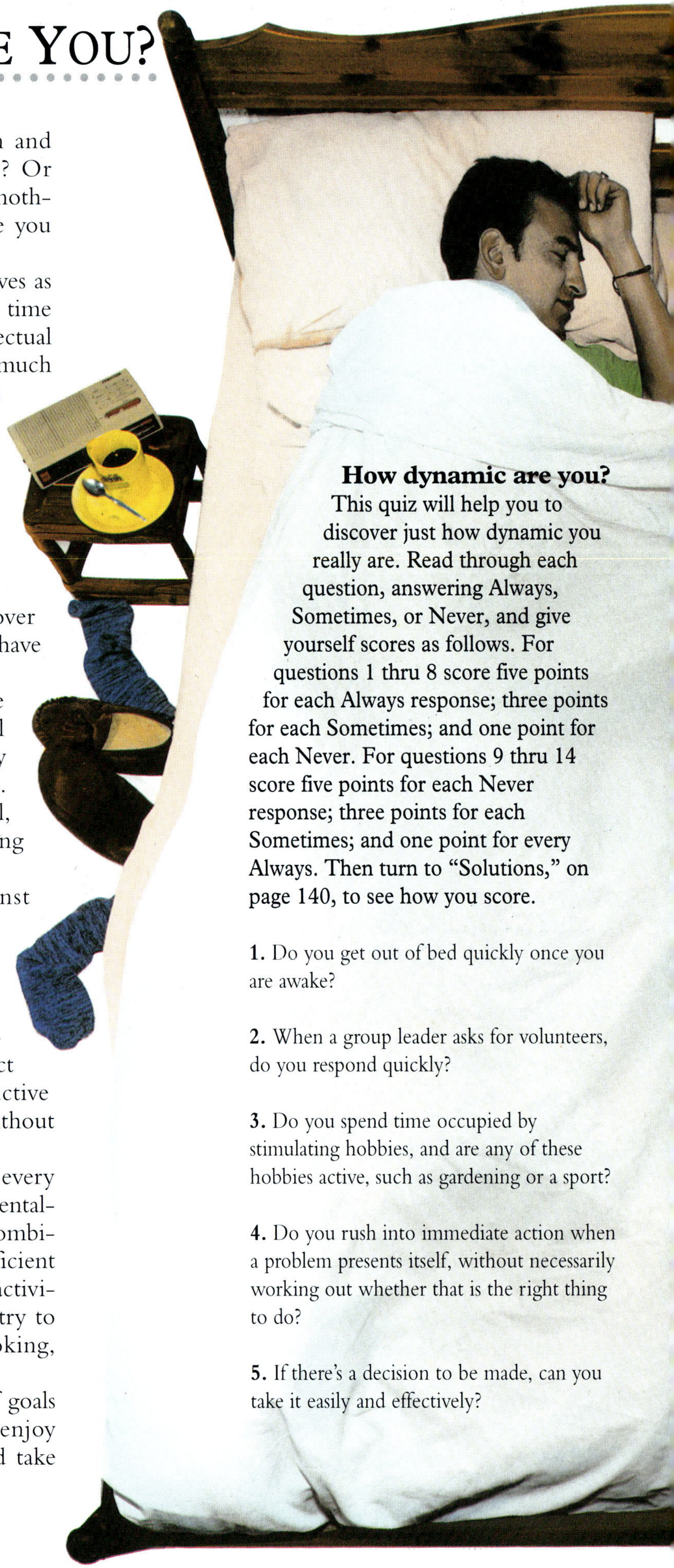

How dynamic are you?

This quiz will help you to discover just how dynamic you really are. Read through each question, answering Always, Sometimes, or Never, and give yourself scores as follows. For questions 1 thru 8 score five points for each Always response; three points for each Sometimes; and one point for each Never. For questions 9 thru 14 score five points for each Never response; three points for each Sometimes; and one point for every Always. Then turn to "Solutions," on page 140, to see how you score.

1. Do you get out of bed quickly once you are awake?

2. When a group leader asks for volunteers, do you respond quickly?

3. Do you spend time occupied by stimulating hobbies, and are any of these hobbies active, such as gardening or a sport?

4. Do you rush into immediate action when a problem presents itself, without necessarily working out whether that is the right thing to do?

5. If there's a decision to be made, can you take it easily and effectively?

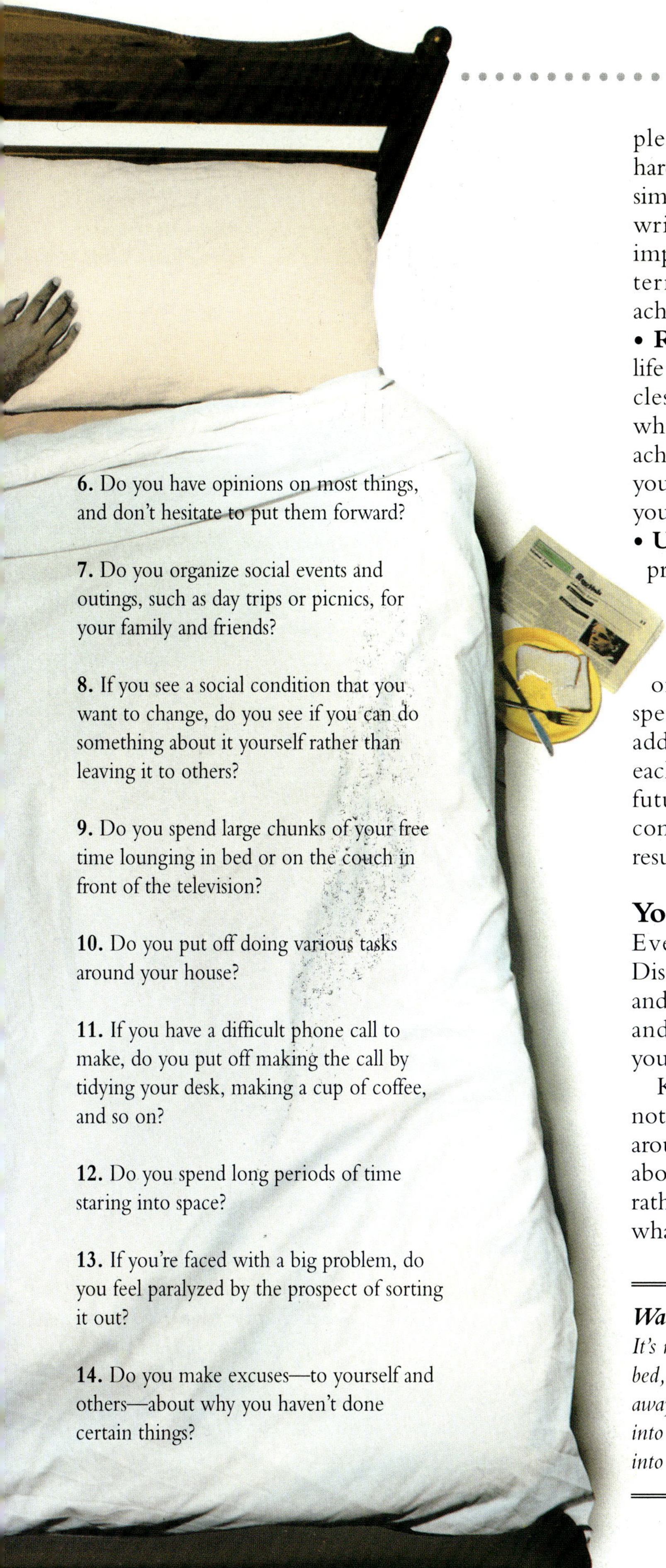

6. Do you have opinions on most things, and don't hesitate to put them forward?

7. Do you organize social events and outings, such as day trips or picnics, for your family and friends?

8. If you see a social condition that you want to change, do you see if you can do something about it yourself rather than leaving it to others?

9. Do you spend large chunks of your free time lounging in bed or on the couch in front of the television?

10. Do you put off doing various tasks around your house?

11. If you have a difficult phone call to make, do you put off making the call by tidying your desk, making a cup of coffee, and so on?

12. Do you spend long periods of time staring into space?

13. If you're faced with a big problem, do you feel paralyzed by the prospect of sorting it out?

14. Do you make excuses—to yourself and others—about why you haven't done certain things?

pleasure in will always encourage you to work harder than those in which you have no interest, or simply feel that you *should* do. It might help if you write your goals down, listing them in order of importance, say, or sorting out which are long-term goals and which you would really like to achieve in the short or medium term.

- **Reevaluate your life.** If you aren't leading the life that you want, try to identify the main obstacles that are standing in your way. Do you fear what might happen if you did take steps toward achieving your aims? Working out the reasons for your inactivity may help give you the impetus that you need to change.
- **Use action-planning strategies.** Cut daunting problems down to size by carving them up into small sections that are easier to manage. When searching for a new job, for instance, take a step-by-step approach. Write down the names of the employment agencies in your area that specialize in your chosen field, along with their address and telephone number. Call or write to each of them enquiring about current vacancies or future prospects, and then make a list of useful contacts and likely positions. Finally update your resumé and run off plenty of copies.

You're the boss

Everyone has hidden reserves of dynamism. Discovering these and then using them to change and improve the quality of your life, are the first and biggest steps you can take toward fulfilling your potential.

Keep in mind, though, that being dynamic does not mean that you have to be constantly rushing around in a frenzy—genuine dynamism is basically about being in total control of your own destiny rather than passively waiting for, and reacting to, whatever fate sends your way.

Wake up!

It's never too late to get out of bed, turn off the televison, clear away the clutter—and spring into action to turn your dreams into reality.

Making a Life Plan

WHAT WILL YOUR LIFE be like in a year from now? In three years? In five? Many of us drift through our lives without planning any further ahead than our next vacation. Like actors standing in the wings, we wait to be handed a script and for a voice offstage to shout "Action!"—and meanwhile life passes us by. But it is never too late to be your own director and decide what you want from your life. Actively plotting its path helps you do this, making sure that, as far as is possible, everything you do moves you nearer to your goals and dreams.

Getting there step by step

Setting yourself small goals on the way to achieving your life plan means that you have concrete steps moving you along your way—as well as showing you how you are progressing. For instance, you don't become a star performer overnight. It takes a succession of steps, the most important of which is practice.

Make your dreams reality

It is important for your life plan to be written down. This is not simply so you remember it; mapping out your plan on paper gives your hopes and ambitions form, and makes them tangible. So long as your goals exist only in your thoughts, you may find it hard to focus your attention and energy on working toward them because it is too easy to dismiss them and tell yourself, "It was just an idea. I'm not all that bothered." Writing down your plan makes your commitment to yourself and your goals more important, so you make greater efforts to get what you want. A more detailed guide to making a life plan appears over the page.

Many people don't follow their dreams and aim for what they want because they tell themselves that it's impossible and that they'll never achieve it. This is why identifying the stages on the way to your goal, and being specific about the actions you need to take, is so helpful. Then, you will be able to figure out the best ways to move at every point.

Firstly, buy the basic tools of your craft, investing as much money as you possibly can in them.

Then, surround yourself with acknowledged experts in that field. In the case of music, this means listening to the best musicians on good quality equipment.

WHY MAKE A LIFE PLAN?

Perhaps you feel you don't need to make a plan because you know what you want. But making a plan will help you define the steps you need to take in order to achieve your goals. It works as follows:

- Helps you define your goals and priorities, especially those which have been unclear to you.
- Breaks down "impossible" dreams into smaller, more achievable stages.
- Gives you a sense of direction, so you actively aim for something, rather than responding to events.
- Helps you acknowledge all your ambitions and dreams so you avoid the frustration of suppressing unrecognized parts of your real self.
- Makes your goals more realistic and tangible so that they inspire you rather than making you feel they're too far beyond your reach.
- Identifies stages of progress so you know what is your next course of action.
- Makes you think about what you really want in each area of your life so that you become more fulfilled in general, and a happy, balanced person.
- Helps you visualize yourself as you want to be, which enforces a positive attitude and, therefore, makes success more likely.

Some people feel that planning is too clinical, or precludes spontaneity. This is not true; in fact, having a plan makes it easier to be spontaneous and to take risks because you are working toward the things you really want. Without a life plan, there is a danger that you will simply react to the actions of others. With a life plan, you are taking charge of your life, not drifting aimlessly.

The third step should be to practice as much as you possibly can. Work hard at gaining mastery of your craft.

Then, having done all you need to prepare yourself for your goal, you will be in a position to actually try for it.

How to Make a Life Plan

You may already have quite a clear idea in your head of what your life plan for the next few years is, but, even if you do, first write down what your complete fantasy is about and how you would like your life to be in, say, five years' time. The only restriction when you are making this plan is that your fantasy life can't depend entirely on luck.

Try to include how you would like the major elements of your life to be—such as career, relationship, family, lifestyle, and interests. For example, Michael, a 32-year-old marketing manager, has a fantasy like this: "I'll have built up my own small business offering marketing advice and strategies. I'll be in a stable, close relationship with someone who is funny and creative, as well as being successful in her own right. We'll have an old house on the coast, which we'll restore and decorate, and I'll also have enough time to create a beautiful garden and to learn how to play the guitar."

Breaking up the fantasy into its components may help you see that some parts are more attainable than you thought. You could start working on these short-term goals at the same time as making plans for achieving your long-term goals. For example, Michael needs to make long-range plans for setting up his business and establishing a stable relationship; in the short term, he could begin guitar lessons and investigate the possibility of moving to

	Goals	**First step**	**Sub-goal 1**	**Sub-goal 2**	**Progress made**
Career/work 	*Find more interesting and challenging work, perhaps in personnel or training? Eventually, attain managerial position in one of these spheres.*	*Check if any suitable openings or training courses are available at work. Ask personnel department—but also look informally, making contact with people who are doing what I want to do.*	*Apply for transfer to Head Office where course opportunities are available and request on-the-job training. Give them clear ideas of what I'd like to do.*	*Move to company with extensive in-house training program. Get newspapers and relevant journals to research state of job market.*	*Checked with personnel. No openings at present, but training may be available next year. That's much too long to wait.*
Relationship 	*Spend more leisure time together as a couple, doing a variety of activities that will bring the two of us closer together.*	*Discuss with Colin on next quiet evening in (Thursday) how we could make more time together and how best to use it.*	*Have long chat with Colin; discuss our relationship and how we feel about it in general; set specific goals after this discussion.*		*Discussed with Colin on Thursday. Decided to try going on cycle rides in countryside every Saturday afternoon, starting tomorrow!*
Interests 	*1. Learn how to speak Italian.* *2. Develop my interest in music, perhaps in a more active way.*	*1. Phone local colleges to enquire about adult education courses available.* *2. Join music appreciation society—one that covers a wide variety of music.*	*1. Sign up for beginner's Italian.* *2. Go to a classical music concert at least once a month.*	*1. Be able to order a meal in a restaurant on holiday in Rome, and hold brief conversations in hotels.* *2. Organize a "music swap" circle to share music and expand tastes.*	*1. Found out about availability of classes; booked for next term. Bought language tape to get me started.* *2. Sent off form for music society. Got brochure from concert hall to book events.*

a house with a bigger garden. His plan could be organized in a similar way to the one drawn up by Rachel (below), a graduate in her 20s who wanted a clearer sense of direction both in her professional life and her relationship with her partner Colin.

Be specific: Don't just think "I want to be successful" or "I want to be happily married"; make your plans detailed and concrete. Write down the steps you need to take to achieve what you want. It is particularly important to identify the first step toward each goal, and commit yourself to taking it. Take a look at Rachel's sample plan to give you an idea of what yours might look like. You might add other columns—like social life, health, and so on.

It is also helpful to put down sub-goals which are steps toward your main aim. Attaining these sub-goals will help you to tell whether or not you are on track, how fast you are traveling toward your larger ambitions—and will give you a sense of achievement when you reach those goals.

While planning cannot guarantee a good outcome—whether it's for a party, a career move, or any other area of your life—it can certainly significantly increase your chances of success. What it does is strengthen the underlying movement toward your goals so that, even when there are the inevitable hitches, setbacks, and diversions, it is relatively easy for you to get back on course.

	Goals	First step	Sub-goal 1	Sub-goal 2	Progress made
Family 	*Have more social occasions that include our immediate families, both in order to have a good time and for us all to overcome longstanding resentments.*	*Phone both sets of parents to sound them out about my idea.*	*Organize family party for the end of next month with "pot-luck" supper. Make sure all of the family agree to come.*	*Have regular get-togethers, with each of us in turn hosting a large event. Everyone able to express feelings spontaneously, and still remain friends.*	*Spoke to others. First family party at our place on 23rd. Dad organizing barbecue month after next at his house.*
Lifestyle/home 	*1. Get fitter, so that I can increase my muscle tone for the beach next summer, and run around with the kids.* *2. Brighten up kitchen and bathroom.*	*1. Go to local gym and have fitness assessment.* *2. Speak to Colin about ideas/finances. Could we repaint or lay new flooring?*	*1. Walk to work one day a week.* *2. Repaint kitchen; get brochures of new bathroom equipment and buy home decorating magazines.*	*1. Organize weekly aerobics class near office for lunchtime or after work.* *2. Have new flooring laid in lighter color. Find cheap and cheerful temporary bathroom decorations.*	*1. Walked to work on Tuesday. Booked appointment at gym. Asked boss if we can use basement for aerobics class. Said yes!* *2. Bought yellow paint. Two days off to paint kitchen.*
Personal development 	*Be able to speak my mind more and voice my opinions. Be more assertive, and be able to say no when I would like to, without feeling guilty.*	*Next time I disagree at work or with family, I will give my opinion without criticizing theirs.*	*Get more involved in decision-making at work and at home. Put forward ideas, and feel comfortable when people don't agree with them.*	*Be able to ask for what I want instead of expecting others to know and then resenting them when they don't.*	*Disagreed with colleague on Monday. He tried to interrupt me, but I stood my ground. Felt nervous, but survived!*

TAKING RISKS

Life is a risky business. Many of the most enjoyable things that it has to offer—forming relationships and friendships, learning new skills, traveling to different countries, expanding our abilities in a new job—involve risk of some kind. Without taking risks, you cannot progress, and you cannot make the most of your life or of yourself. But, despite the fact that taking certain kinds of risk offers the possibility of a life that is more rewarding and fulfilling, many people shun such opportunities at all costs, allowing that all-purpose get-out clause "But what if..." to cheat them of the possible rewards.

What's stopping you?

People avoid taking risks for many reasons, but perhaps the most common ones are habit, inertia, and fear.

Habit probably governs your life more than you would care to admit; in many areas, you use habit for convenience or ease—you get so used to driving to work that you do it without even thinking about it, so why change to cycling or using public transportation instead? However, you also use habitual behavior because it is familiar and so makes you feel safe. For example, you may remain in an unhappy relationship because at least you know what to expect.

Inertia can be equally insidious and sometimes becomes a habit in itself. Far too often, it may seem easier just to drift through life and take things as they come, rather than actively going out and taking responsibility for making your life what it is.

Fear holds most of us back at some time in our lives. For example, suppose you were invited to a party on your own. Your first response might be to make an excuse because you are worried that you won't know anyone there. But if you really want to meet people, where are you more likely to find them—at the party, or sitting at home watching TV? Try to acknowledge your fear—but not give in to it. Actually, many of our imagined fears have little rational basis. Once at the party, you might see a group of interesting-looking people you would like to meet, but instead you hold back because you are frightened of how they might react if you were to join in their conversation. You tell yourself "They'll think I'm pushy," or "They won't want to

A distorted view

Don't let irrational fears give you such a nightmarish view of life that you would always choose staying at home over going to a party and meeting new people.

talk to me." In fact, many people at the party will be feeling exactly the same as you. When you are locked into this kind of defeatist thinking, you need to break the pattern, in this case perhaps by deciding to enter into the discussion when the topic of conversation is something that you are confidently familiar with.

Breaking "safe" patterns

When you are in a situation that makes you anxious because you think it is risky, remember that this edgy feeling can also indicate that you find the prospect quite exciting. Don't let this put you off; simply allow yourself to feel nervous to begin with. Then ask yourself the following questions:

1. What is the worst thing that might happen?
2. Could I live with that?
3. If it did happen, what would my next step be?
4. How can I maximize the likelihood of a good outcome, and minimize that of a bad one?

Once you allow yourself to fantasize about the worst thing that might happen, you often realize that it is not really as frightening as you first thought—and that if it did happen, you could actually deal with it. The visualization techniques outlined on pages 34-37 will help you to build your confidence and improve your ability to deal with all types of things, by using your imagination to explore different emotions and possible outcomes in any situation.

In order to break out of safe patterns, you may also need to change your "self-talk": that nagging internal voice that gives you a million reasons why you can't do something. Start consciously repeating positive messages to yourself and you may find that this is a habit that soon becomes automatic—a habit that will help you move mountains.

No regrets

Think back over your life. On the whole, have you regretted things that you *did*, or things that you *didn't* do? Most people regret the missed opportunities, the things they didn't do. In later life, regrets will offer you little comfort, so it makes sense to reduce your causes for regret. Taking risks—to retrain for a different career, to allow other people to get close to you, to commit yourself to pursuing your goals—expands enormously the potential for joy. Dare to live a little, and you'll probably find yourself living a lot.

BRAVE—OR RASH?

Taking risks in your life is not about behaving rashly or plunging into unknown situations without forethought. There is a world of difference between acting rashly or dangerously because you are denying the presence of risk, and acknowledging and understanding the risk before choosing your course of action. For example, if you wanted to leave your job and set up your own business, you would need to devote a certain amount of time and energy in advance to:

- assessing what demand there is for the product or service you want to offer
- estimating your overheads
- deciding how to market yourself, and so on

You might then decide to take the risk and leave your job. By contrast, it would probably be rash just to walk out of your job one day and then start wondering how you might set up a business.

The best plan is to build up your willingness and ability to take risks gradually—there is no need to plunge in at the deep end. Try practicing first in areas that matter less to you, or aim to tackle new challenges in stages, so that your overall confidence steadily increases.

Start small
You don't need to start out by diving right down to the sea-bed to find your treasure. Begin more cautiously by dipping a toe in new waters.

DECISION-MAKING

Imagine what life would be like if you were totally indecisive about everything: Even getting ready in the morning would be an ordeal—should you take a bath or a shower? This example might seem ridiculous, but many people impede their chances of success with this kind of indecision. Why waste your life mentally shifting from foot to foot? You have the capacity to be more decisive and to make decisions that are right for you.

Decide to succeed

Why is decisiveness so important for success? As well as making life run more smoothly, it also:

- allows you to put your plans into action
- lets you commit to and move toward your goals
- helps you actively take charge of your life
- stops you from getting stuck in a rut

When making decisions, keep your sights set on your overall goal. Ask yourself: "What do I want to achieve?" and "How could this decision help me achieve it?" As well as pointing you toward the best course of action, this will render you less likely to be sidetracked by unimportant information, particularly when you need to undertake research in order to make a decision. Also examine the way you feel about the issue and the emotions it raises: this can direct you to a satisfying decision.

Combat indecision

Many people who feel they are generally indecisive have little trouble making effective decisions in some areas of their lives. For example, you might find it hard to decide on a plan of action at work, but have no trouble deciding how best to raise your children.

You may believe that this is because you have more experience or expertise in a certain area. More often, however, it stems mainly from a lack of confidence, especially if you have had your

On the right track
Working out a clear decision-making strategy will help you to choose the right road.

self-confidence undermined early on in life by an overcritical teacher or parent. The next time you have to make a tough decision, picture yourself making a good decision in an area in which you have more confidence. Imagine the processes you would go through, what factors you would take into account, and then how you would feel at each stage. Now apply these procedures to the problematic issue concerned.

Weigh up the pros and cons

The following exercise can be a very effective decision-making tool. On a piece of paper, make a column for each possible option. Now divide each column in two, one half headed For, the other Against. List the pros and cons for each option, grading each one from 1 to 10 (1=relatively unimportant, 10=extremely important.) Add up the pro and con score for each, then minus the con score from the pro one. The highest score should be your best option. If you still feel unsure, then maybe it's time to explore your gut reactions further.

Jump ahead

Another useful technique is to pick any of the options you are considering and imagine that you have already chosen it as your decision. What would your next act be? How would you implement your decision? How would it help you progress toward your overall goal? How does it make you feel? Putting yourself one step further along the way helps you to understand the implications of your decision and how you really feel about the possible outcomes.

Succeed step by step

Where you have adequate information at your disposal, a logical, step-by-step decision-making process can be invaluable in highlighting the best option:

1. **Define** the dilemma that requires a decision.
2. **State** your aim or goal.
3. **Outline** options that might achieve this aim.
4. **Specify** vital criteria.
5. **Assess** options in relation to the vital criteria.
6. **Implement** your choice.
7. **Monitor** the outcome. Did your choice help you achieve your goal and fulfill additional criteria?

Take responsibility

You won't necessarily always make the "right" decision. What is important is to turn a problem situation into a positive one, and to do that, you need to:

- **Take responsibility for your decision:** Do not apportion blame elsewhere or bury the mistake. Accept that you are human and, therefore, fallible.
- **Assess the nature and extent of the problem:** Is it really so awful, or just not what you had expected? Does it throw up any good points?
- **Explore constructive ways to proceed:** You don't have to stick with what you've got just because you expended energy making your original decision.
- **Learn from the experience:** Don't just dismiss a "wrong" decision as bad luck—there is little that cannot be used as helpful information for the future.

Logic Versus Intuition

There are two main decision-making approaches that people use: the rational or **strategic approach** and the "gut feeling" or **intuitive approach**. Each has its advantages, but neither should be used exclusively. Which one you use most is often governed by natural preference. It is important to be flexible, however, and tailor your approach to the situation; a combination of the two approaches, weaving together a solution you are most comfortable with, is frequently highly effective.

- **The strategic approach.** This relies on following a logical series of steps, researching and analyzing relevant information, defining criteria to be met, assessing each option against the overall aim, taking negative factors into account, and eliminating the least satisfactory options.

- **The intuitive approach.** This means looking at the situation from a different perspective, allowing imagination and creativity free rein, tuning in to gut reaction, keeping the whole picture in mind rather than homing in on details, questioning established practices and assumptions, and rejecting options that don't "feel" right.

WHOSE RESPONSIBILITY IS IT?

Having the confidence to accept responsibility for past or present predicaments instead of blaming others or feeling that you are not in a position to change your circumstances requires an active rather than passive approach to life.

To find out whether you need to become more active in deciding what happens to you, ask yourself the following questions. Be as honest as you possibly can. Then turn to "Solutions," on page 140, to help you assess your answers.

1. When considering your past do/did you:
a) blame all of your shortcomings on your parents?
b) feel you are the way you are due to your genetic make-up, and there is nothing you can do to change?
c) realize that there are some things about yourself that you need to change but that you might also need counseling to help you do it?

2. You've failed to get the promotion that you had hoped for. Do you:
a) feel furious at your boss or manager and immediately think about looking for another job?
b) feel deeply hurt and rejected, but assume it is for the best because you probably didn't deserve the promotion anyway?
c) make an appointment to see your boss to discuss why you weren't promoted and also to talk about ways of improving your performance?

3. At work, you've missed a vital deadline and lost a very important client. Do you:
a) blame the other people who were involved and the faulty equipment, as well as complain that the schedule was completely unrealistic to begin with?
b) contemplate quitting your job because you've always felt that you weren't really cut out for it?
c) meet with your boss to analyze reasons for the delay, accepting responsibility for areas that were definitely your fault or where you had control?

4. You find your present job deeply unsatisfying and dull, and you respond by thinking:
a) I'll hand in my notice and travel for six months.
b) even though I'm unhappy there's really nothing else that I am qualified to do, so I guess I'm stuck.
c) maybe I need to think about getting more useful skills or even changing careers.

5. Your phone has been cut off because the bill hasn't been paid. Do you react by:
a) contacting the phone company and insisting that you never received the bills (a lie) and that it must be the postal service's problem?
b) feeling too embarrassed to admit that you haven't paid the phone bill because you are having financial difficulties?
c) explaining to the phone company that you are having money problems and apologize for not speaking to them sooner. You also meet with a financial adviser to help you budget more sensibly?

6. The worst argument you have ever had with your best friend ends with the two of you being unusually angry with each other and not speaking for weeks. Do you:
a) refuse to contact or even speak with your friend until he or she apologizes?
b) feel guilty and foolish, and arrange for a large bouquet of flowers and a box of chocolates to be sent to your friend at work?
c) wait until you have cooled down and then call your friend and suggest that the two of you meet to discuss rationally what happened, bearing in mind that there was probably blame on both parts?

7. Your relationships always end after a few months. Your attitude is that:
a) I've just been terribly unlucky. Everyone with whom I have ever had a relationship has turned out to be unreliable or a jerk.
b) I'm useless. It's got to be me. I'm just not meant to have a relationship.
c) maybe I'm doing something wrong, but there may be other things going on also. I need to think seriously about why this keeps happening.

8. You've recently started dating the person of your dreams. Do you think:
a) fate has brought us together; this relationship is definitely meant to be.
b) this is too good to be true, but wait till he or she finds out what I'm really like. He or she won't stay a minute.
c) I'll enjoy this now, while I've got it. I don't know what will happen in the future, or what I'll be feeling, but I hope we'll be together.

9. You've just discovered that your partner has been unfaithful. Do you:
a) confront your lover with anger and tears, and accuse him or her of being the worst person who has ever lived?
b) feel crushed and humiliated—it must be your fault?
c) arrange to talk to your partner, as painful as it will be, and try to find out what's happening and why?

10. You're ten pounds overweight and have been for a while. Do you think:
a) this is the way I am. There's no point fighting it?
b) I'd like to lose weight, but I'm too weak-willed to do it?
c) I find dieting difficult to maintain, but I will seek help, maybe from a support group?

11. You've had colds all winter, and your friends say you look pale and drawn. You react by:
a) wondering why you're feeling so tired all the time: could it be that others have made you take on too much work, too many chores, etc.
b) worrying that you could be seriously ill, but don't want to bother your doctor.
c) admitting that you eat badly, don't get enough sleep, and drink too much alcohol. You realize that you need to change and will seek help.

12. If someone close to you suggests you stop smoking and cut down on alcohol, do you think:
a) I would like to cut down but my friends pressure me to drink and smoke more.
b) what's the point? I've done it too long for it to make any difference to my health if I stop now.
c) what I'm currently doing is self-destructive and I must make the effort to change my behavior.

The luck of the draw

Everyone has problems to overcome, and this will involve difficulties over which you may feel powerless. But to take control of your life and to do what's best for you, you need to figure out what is your responsibility, and what is down to other people.

PROFESSIONAL TACTICS

COMMUNICATION IS THE BRIDGE between you and the outside world, covering every aspect of the messages you send out and receive. One of the foundation stones of success in any area of life is the ability to communicate well. As well as enabling you to get across your ideas and plans, it inspires others' confidence in your capabilities, helps you make the most of all your relationships, and smooths your progress through life.

Clear signals

Communication is a two-way process—the more attention you pay to the feedback you get from other people, the more effective a communicator you will become. Suppose you send your friend a note and she complains that she can't read it. The fault may lie with your handwriting, with your friend's ability to decipher it, or with both, but remember that if people aren't receiving your message, then it's up to you, as the communicator, to transmit a clearer signal. Don't expect people to understand what you mean just because *you* do. Consider these five golden rules:

1. Be clear. Is it possible that you could be easily misunderstood? If in doubt, make sure you opt for clarity over cleverness every time. Also, be quite clear with yourself about what it is that you want to achieve from your communication, or you will achieve very little.

2. Be direct. Are you open about what you think, what you want, and what your aims are?

3. Be appropriate. The context, including who is at the receiving end of your communication, will influence how you deliver your message. Getting this right will make your task much easier.

4. Be relevant. Stick to the point. Becoming sidetracked weakens the impact of your message and makes it easier for people not to take you seriously.

5. Be attentive. Pay attention to feedback. Have your listeners understood you? If you are asked to repeat yourself several times, perhaps you are not coming across well enough. Ask a few pertinent questions to test whether or not you are being understood. Is your audience paying attention? How could you make them more involved and interested?

The force of feedback

Other people are constantly giving out signals that can help you understand how they respond to you. As well as listening to what they say directly, stay attuned to non-verbal messages. Constant glances

SAY IT WITHOUT WORDS

Studies show that if you are making a presentation to a group, only about 7 percent of the impression you make stems from the actual content of the presentation. Of the remainder, 38 percent comes from the tone of your voice, and 55 percent from your non-verbal communication—your body language and posture, eye contact, and so on. If you are to get your meaning across successfully, then both your verbal and non-verbal messages need to complement each other at all times. For instance, imagine if someone in a court trial entered the witness box and, while swearing to tell the truth, shifted from foot to foot, fiddled with his tie, and looked down at the floor. Which of these messages would you be likely to trust the most—the verbal message or the non-verbal one?

The right image
Your body language and appearance should show you in a positive light.

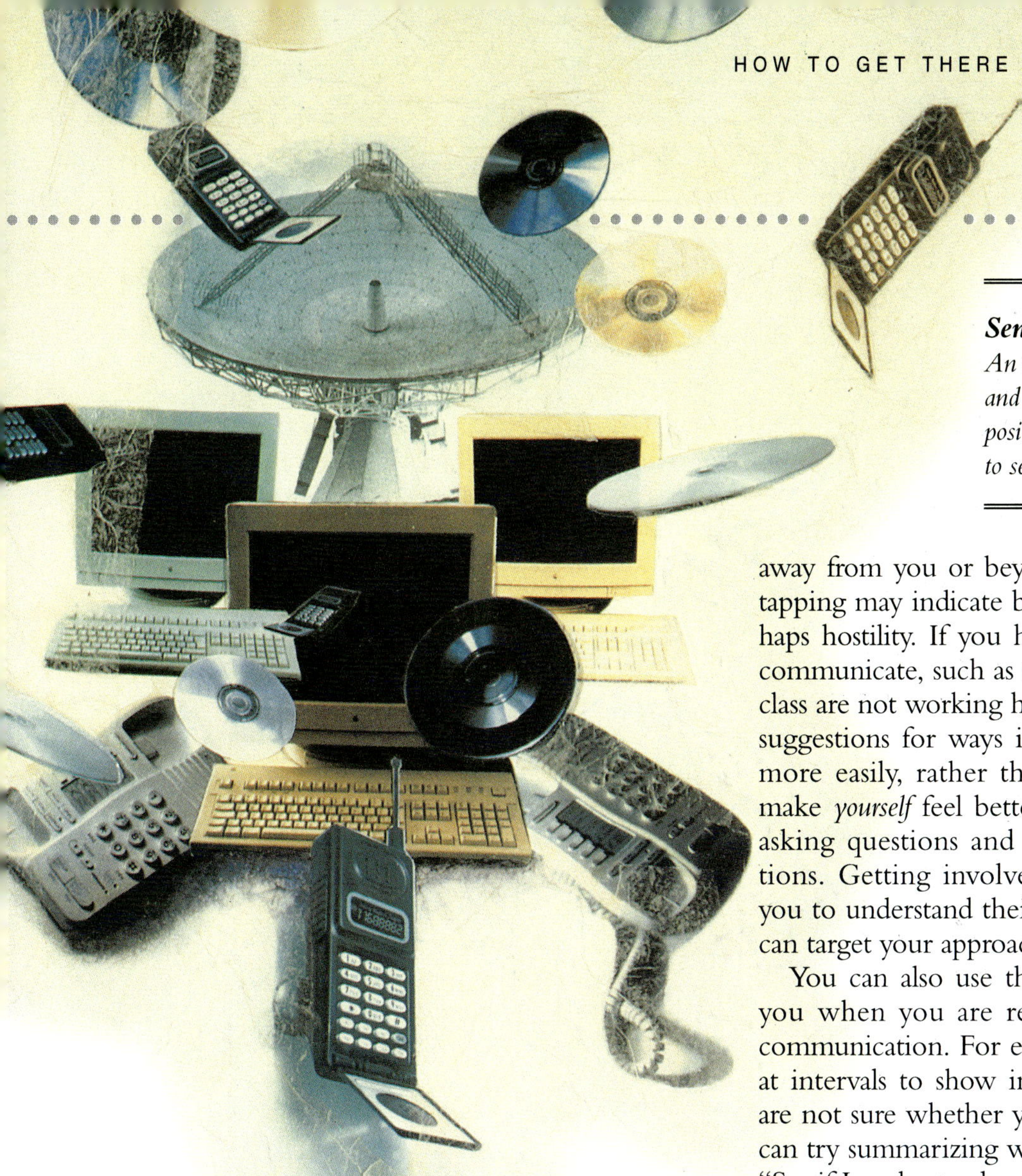

Sending out a clear signal
An understanding of yourself and others, and of how to put yourself across positively, is the basic equipment you need to send out clear messages.

away from you or beyond you, fidgeting, and foot-tapping may indicate boredom, impatience—or perhaps hostility. If you have something unpalatable to communicate, such as the fact that the pupils in your class are not working hard enough, offer constructive suggestions for ways in which they might progress more easily, rather than blowing a fuse simply to make *yourself* feel better. Draw your listeners in, by asking questions and encouraging their contributions. Getting involved with your audience helps you to understand their responses better, so that you can target your approach more precisely.

You can also use the power of feedback to help you when you are responding to someone else's communication. For example, lean forward and nod at intervals to show interest and agreement. If you are not sure whether you have understood fully, you can try summarizing what you think has been stated: "So, if I understand you correctly, you think the best way to proceed is...?"

Projecting a positive image

If you show yourself in a positive light, others will respond accordingly. This doesn't mean being arrogant; what it does entail is:

- Making it clear that you are capable and confident.
- Being direct about your aims and proposed actions.
- Stressing the positive aspects of your intentions.
- Acknowledging potential problems and making it appear clear to everyone that you can handle them; perhaps referring to previous situations where you have handled things well.
- Using language clearly, avoiding terms that you think may not be understood easily.
- Appreciating the contributions and help of others.

Above all, positive communicators know exactly what it is they are trying to get across. They also know themselves and how they work—because if you can't understand your own feelings, thoughts, and responses, you will have fallen at the first fence.

You can help yourself make a good impression by remembering the following points:

- Make sure that your body language doesn't detract from or contradict what you are saying. If you want to emphasize the fact that you are open, direct, and confident, keep an open body position—without folding your arms or crossing your legs.
- Use hand gestures to add emphasis and vitality to what you are saying, and take care not to cover your mouth with your hand, as this sends the message "I'm not sure I believe what I'm saying."
- Adopt whatever style, in terms of general manner and dress, you feel reflects the image you have of yourself as a successful person (see "Looking the Part," pp. 94-95). However, don't put yourself on a pedestal—that does not help communication.

Influencing Others

Most successful managers and business leaders are extremely skilled in the art of communicating successfully. This is because those whose responsibilities include managing others need to be able to listen to and motivate their staff. Whether you are striving for success in the workplace, or merely wanting to improve the quality of communication with your family or friends, motivation and self-assertion techniques will help.

Dealing successfully with people and getting them to do what you want involves more than just good comunication (see "Professional Tactics," p. 86). It requires various qualities including the ability to motivate and inspire, as well as knowing how to be assertive without being unduly aggressive. The real key to influencing others, however, is respect. To command respect you must first demonstrate a clear appreciation of what it means to be honest, loyal, and compassionate. But even then the granting of respect is not immediate. It has to be earned gradually over a period of time through your character and the consistency of your actions.

Learn to assert yourself

To be respected you first need to learn how to voice your own wishes and opinions in such a way that other people are clear about your meaning but don't feel intimidated. These are the techniques of assertion.

- **Use "I" rather** than "you." If something bothers you, state your own feelings directly rather than attacking the other person. For example, "I found the way you interrupted me when I was speaking very distracting," is far better than "You are always interrupting me," which tends to inspire defensiveness and is unlikely to result in change.
- **Learn to say** "no." Don't be brow-beaten into doing something that you don't want to do. Learn how to say no, even when the other person persists in trying to persuade you to change your mind. Use the technique of the "broken record." Continue to repeat your refusal, without being distracted by the other person's attempts to persuade you.

- **Recognize the other's** point of view, but stick to your own. In the interests of being nice and avoiding arguments, there are some people who agree with everybody. In the short term, this may keep the peace, but people who agree with everyone get credit from no one. Hold your own opinions and express them with confidence. Listen to others' views and, if you disagree, don't be afraid to say so. But always speak respectfully so other people realize it is only their opinion that is being disagreed with.
- **Don't be afraid** to admit your mistakes and apologize. There is a school of thought that says "Never apologize, never explain." But there are also many people nursing grievances that could easily be dispelled if someone had the good grace and the magnanimity to apologize for what had happened.

How to Motivate Others

How do you motivate others successfully, especially to take on tasks they don't want—for example, getting your child to tidy his room, or recruiting a member of staff to work overtime in order to meet a deadline? There are basically two approaches to motivating others: using the "stick" or the "carrot." The former approach uses harsh commands or threats to get the person moving. The other, more successful, motivational approach relies on incentives that involve encouraging creativity, praising work that has been done well, and urging people to act responsibly on their own initiative in order to complete a task successfully. In other words, this approach uses the carrot to motivate others.

Empathizing with others

To gain the respect of someone else, you must first make sure that he or she feels valued. In other words, when a person feels devalued, his or her performance is usually poor. However, when a person feels valued, he or she is generally cooperative, and eager to strive for success. To help people feel valued, try praising them—without sounding patronizing—and giving them tasks that are challenging and important but not overwhelming or demoralizing.

If you are in a position to oversee the work of other people, inevitably there will be times when you have to give constructive criticism. Good criticism instills the message that you value the person and believe him or her capable of much more. One trick of motivating someone successfully through criticism is to mix the criticism with praise.

Pulling together

Successful motivators will be able to get the best out of others, and help them make up a united, constructive team.

Mucking in

You will never be able to motivate or influence other people—or gain their respect—if they have the impression that you feel the task in question is beneath you. Convincing others that you believe yourself to be a part of the group, regardless of your status, is important not just for strengthening the general atmosphere of comradeship, but also for establishing team spirit. Willingness on your part to attempt any appropriate task will help to instill respect and encourage the others to work toward success. In other words, never ask someone else to do something you aren't prepared to do yourself—whatever your status.

Listening constructively

Learn how to listen successfully to other people. Listening is the basic skill that underlies all other social skills. This is because unless you understand the position or point of view of the other person, you will not be able to focus your communication to maximum effect.

Know your listening weaknesses. Do you often daydream, interrupt, or assume you know what is going to be said and so switch off? Do you wait impatiently to add your bit, and are you thinking about what you are going to say rather than listening? A good listener gives the person he or she is listening to his or her undivided attention—and knows their contribution is valuable.

Another problem is that feelings or bias always get in the way of understanding. Perhaps you assume that anyone who looks or speaks in a certain way cannot have anything sensible to say? Remember that prejudice can seriously impede effective listening, and it is only by becoming an objective, good listener that you can communicate well and thus motivate other people.

Good Organization

"If you want to make sure a job gets done, give it to a busy person." This maxim is based on the premise that busy people create a sound structure of working routines to help them carry out tasks efficiently—in other words, they are well organized. Effective organization can transform your professional and domestic life by increasing productivity, reducing stress levels, and freeing time for relaxation.

Keep track of time

Before you can learn to employ your time effectively, you first need to find out how it is being spent, and one way of accomplishing this is by keeping a time diary. Start by writing MONDAY at the top of a sheet of paper, and mark down the left-hand edge each hour and half hour of your working day. Then draw up a similar sheet for the rest of the week. Each morning, you should make a list of things you want to accomplish during the day—completing an expenses claim, changing the bedlinen, and so forth. Keep your diary close to hand and jot down truthfully how you spent each half-hour period. What you are likely to discover is the "Pareto principle" in action: that is, 80 percent of work is usually accomplished in 20 percent of the time. Although some nonproductive preparation is necessary for many tasks, you may be surprised to discover how much of your day is taken up with re-arranging ornaments or flicking through magazines. Clawing back some of these wasted hours will help you to achieve more with less anxiety.

Know yourself

Analyzing your time diary can also reveal less obvious personality factors at work: if you're honest, for example, do you find the pressure of an imminent

Pass the Buck

Effective delegation is an essential part of good organization. At work, this may mean relinquishing some parts of your job—mundane tasks such as copying or word-processing, perhaps, or skilled, but self-contained, tasks like research.

At home, it could involve investing in a dishwasher or a microwave oven. Also, parents can assign even small children simple jobs like setting the table, keeping their own room tidy, or taking out the trash.

Implementing these ideas may involve rethinking old habits and operating in unfamiliar ways. Once you establish a structure of effective organization, however, working within it will quickly become second nature.

Vicky and Roger, for instance, are well aware of the advantages of sharing household chores and responsibilities. Both of them have very demanding full-time jobs, and they recognize that it isn't fair to expect all of the domestic tasks to be done by one person alone.

deadline so stimulating that you actually delay starting a job until the last minute? This pattern, although very common, is never satisfactory; no one can work effectively under continuous pressure, and fighting a constant battle with the clock leaves you no room to maneuver in case of unforeseen crises such as equipment malfunction. A related, and equally undesirable, work habit is having several tasks in progress at once and flitting from one to the other. This system may produce the feeling, and the appearance, of being busy but research clearly shows that the most productive work is done in concentrated blocks of time.

Another common problem is the inability to say "no" when you are asked to do a particular job, either because you don't want to let anyone down, or you are afraid of appearing uncooperative. If you can't manage it, say so immediately, rather than opting out when things get out of control.

Sort yourself out
Taking the trouble to organize the various activities and events in your life will reap a wide range of benefits.

If you take on too many obligations—or the wrong ones—there is an obvious, yet often overlooked, option that can work extremely well. When a request is made, most of us want to answer "yes" or "no" right away. Instead, say you need some time—perhaps only an hour—to think about it. Say so politely, firmly, and immediately. It is clear that a decision taken after calm consideration will be more sound than a split-second, often emotionally based, response.

So, they devised a roster whereby the responsibility of most chores would be alternated. For example, on Mondays, Wednesdays, and Fridays Vicky cooks the evening meal, while it is Roger's turn to cook on Tuesdays, Thursdays, and Saturdays. The following week they swap nights, and Sundays are free-for-alls. They have also delegated some tasks to their son, David. It is his responsibility to wash the dishes in the evening and to keep his bedroom clean.

Timely tactics

Some of the most successful aids to good organization are also the simplest. Write out a daily list of tasks, for instance, coded according to their urgency: **A** for "must be completed," **B** for "must progress," and **C** for "can delay." Deal with **A** tasks first, then move on to **B** and **C**. Don't be tempted, though, to leave **C** tasks repeatedly untouched or they may escalate into a crisis.

Invest in a page-a-day diary and record in it jobs to be done as well as appointments. Avoid keeping separate work and social diaries, as the potential for confusion is considerable. Another basic tactic is dealing with routine jobs in clusters, so pay all your bills and write all your letters at the same time. Similarly, doing all the ironing is much quicker than pressing a different outfit each day.

Visual aids can also be helpful. Wall-mounted year planners are a familiar sight in the workplace, where they ensure that staff vacations are staggered. A giant calendar can fulfill a similar function at home, keeping track of events that affect several family members. Or hang up a pinboard to hold messages, receipts, shopping lists, tradesmen's cards, take-out menus, and school notices.

The Successful Image

As soon as we meet new people, we begin to judge them. Some of these judgments are superficial ones about whether they are attractive, well-groomed, stylish, and so forth, but we also make assumptions about character and personality—whether an individual is friendly, intelligent, or trustworthy. This assessment is made solely on the basis of image—the way a person stands, moves, speaks, smiles, and looks at others. Because the effect of these apparently superficial characteristics is so immediate and powerful, they can sometimes be more important even than what we say. However ill-advised and unfair it may be, people do judge books by their cover.

Carry your message

When you don't feel sure of yourself, it's tempting to hang your head, slump your shoulders, and generally try to shrink away out of sight. But no matter how nervous you are, try to conceal your anxiety by standing straight, pulling your shoulders back, and holding your head up. At the same time, take a series of deep breaths and try to relax a little, since a stiff, military stance is as off-putting as a stooped, self-effacing one.

To give an impression of approachability and friendliness, avoid any body-language that creates a barrier between you and others, such as folding your arms across your chest. Try not to wave your arms around in an agitated way. If you are unsure what to do with your arms, try carrying something—a sheaf of papers or files, perhaps, or a notebook. When you're seated, fold your hands on your lap in a relaxed way—white knuckles or nervous hand-wringing will destroy your air of confidence, and can be just as distracting as manic gestures or playing with objects in your hands.

The best way to create a positive impression is by looking calm and confident, since even a veneer of self-assurance goes a long way toward inspiring confidence and approval in others. In turn, when giving the impression of self-assurance elicits a positive response, genuine lasting confidence is much more likely to develop.

Effective packaging
The opinion other people have of you is formed, at least initially, by the image you project through your voice, your posture, and your body language.

The eyes have it

"I don't like him—he has shifty eyes." "Don't trust anyone who can't look you in the eye." These widely-held judgments reflect the important role played by eye contact in all face-to-face communications. To give the right impression, always look directly at the person you're talking to. This suggestion may seem an obvious one, but closing your eyes frequently or letting your gaze wander aimlessly around the room are both common symptoms of nerves. Here too, however, it's vital to avoid extremes, so smile and maintain a steady interested gaze without allowing it to become an unwavering stare; this is guaranteed to unnerve almost anyone.

It ain't what you say

To be able to convey your ideas and wishes to others effectively, your greatest asset will be a pleasant speaking voice—one that is warm and well-modulated, with a fairly low pitch. A foreign or a regional accent need not be a handicap, as long as what you say can be understood without difficulty.

The pitch, tone, and volume of your voice are all indicators of your emotional state, as well as of your general confidence. Soft, slow speech indicates that you are in full control of yourself and the situation; a high-pitched whine, on the other hand, or a bullying shout both suggest a serious lack of control. Even if you are provoked or challenged, try not to get flustered. Stay calm, and deal with the issue in a non-confrontational manner, maybe by repeating or paraphrasing the controversial remark or question to give yourself time to think.

One way of becoming aware of your own voice is by making a recording of it, ideally in the course of a real conversation. You could do this by placing a cassette recorder near the telephone and activating it when you begin to speak. If you have a tendency to sound bossy, hesitant, flat, or shrill, you can work on the problem over several weeks, recording your progress frequently.

When speaking, try to give an impression of confidence by avoiding irritating habits such as leaving frequent long pauses and interjecting meaningless words and phrases such as "um," "sort of," "you know," and "right?" Be careful that anxiety doesn't cause you to speak too quickly; words that come out in a rush are likely to be garbled and incomprehensible, and therefore seriously compromise the effect you are attempting to achieve. Try to be clear about what you want to say before you speak, then be relaxed, cooperative, and sympathetic, but sure of your purpose.

Successful speakers should also be aware of the need to alter the way they communicate to suit different situations and personalities. When briefing or motivating subordinates, you should adopt a short, snappy, and inspirational approach, whereas during a presentation to a group of clients or senior managers, your style is likely to be more measured and statesmanlike. Remember, too, that when you're chatting within a group of people, you should engage everyone in the conversation at some time.

Ask the professionals

Most aspects of the image you project to others can be improved considerably once you become aware of where you have a problem and take a few simple steps toward self-improvement. If you are particularly concerned about your image, however—perhaps because you are about to start, or go after, a new job—look out for one of the many courses available, either on image enhancement as a whole, or on one particular aspect, such as body language, voice production, or public speaking. In addition, professional consultants often work in these areas, giving personal advice on how you can improve your image. This will give you the confidence you need to succeed.

Looking the Part

What you choose to wear makes a statement about you. In the same way, what you choose to wear at work inevitably makes a statement about your attitude to work.

Judging someone by their clothes may seem superficial, but a superficial impression might be the only one that somebody who has a say in your promotion ever gets. A suit, for example, is a way for women and men of many professions to say, "I take my work seriously, I am ambitious and prepared to play things by the book." Where wearing a suit is the norm, someone who chooses to be less formal might appear less confident or less interested in responsibility. Someone who looks smart and very colorful or fashionable, gives a mixture of messages—"I'm me. I'm different. I'm confident. I'm ambitious." This is a helpful image in a profession where there is room for creative flair, but might be a disadvantage in a very conventional bank.

The rules of the game

Many professions, such as nursing or the police force, have their own uniforms. These are often designed for very practical reasons but also help the lay person to identify these professionals more easily. However, most professions have an unspoken dress code that it is equally important to follow if you wish to fit in and be taken seriously. If you don't, you may create the impression that you haven't quite understood the nature of the job.

You may feel that a person should be judged solely on ability, but imagine how you would feel if your lawyer turned up for a hot day in court dressed in shorts and a T-shirt? However brilliant you knew her to be, her choice of clothes might lead you to doubt her grasp of the situation. You might also feel that she was putting her comfort before your case. Few people are so talented that they can challenge the rules of the image game.

You should not underdress at work—it may create an impression that you do not aspire to anything better. However, overdressing can be inappropriate, too. Customers in an outdoor sports shop are likely to assume that an assistant wearing a lumberjack shirt and jeans has better product knowledge than someone wearing a smart suit. They may well find the more casual assistant more approachable, too. The most important thing is to dress appropriately, and take your cue as to what this is from your fellow workers. For instance, if jeans and shirts are the norm, then you would not be perceived as an equal part of the team if you wore a pin-striped suit.

There are some rules about what you should wear at work which should not be broken. Dressing in an overtly sexual manner is never admissible. Clothes that are too tight or short or

Make the right impression

Take your image apart and work out which elements let you down. Then you can start to create the new-look you.

low-cut, and T-shirts with sexual slogans on them, will always give the wrong message. Dressing practically is also important: many women wear high heels to work—but take care that you can walk in them. All-white outfits can look very good at the beginning of the day, but in many environments, they will lose their freshness very quickly. Make sure that you are comfortable—you won't do good work if you are too hot or can't breathe.

Rules for a good wardrobe

Here are a few points to bear in mind when creating the image of the new-look you. First of all, beware of buying clothes because they look great on somebody else—they may look very different on you. If you have any doubts about whether something suits you, don't buy it. Wait a few days, then try it on again and see what you think. Most of us have an idea of what kind of clothes really suit us—these are the clothes that we prefer to wear and feel most comfortable in. Only buy clothes that fit you well, and never wear clothes that are too tight, particularly if you are trying to lose weight. Instead, find shapes that flatter your figure as it is now.

It is worth investing money in one or two basic classics that will always look smart, whatever the occasion. For example, a stylish raincoat will look good all year round. Similarly, a simple, classic suit is useful for all sorts of smart occasions and will not date.

Look neat and tidy

Good grooming is always important at work, as it is in every other part of your life. Caring for what you wear can make a big difference to your appearance, too. Your clothes, like your hair, nails, and shoes, should look clean and tidy. When you buy, pay attention to the care labels. Are you prepared for the expense of dry cleaning every time you wear something? If the label says "hand wash with care," consider whether you can really spare the time to do this. Beware of fabrics that crease easily, because unless you can carry off the fashionably creased look it tends to look rather unkempt. Stay away from synthetics, particularly if you work in a hot and close place, and buy clothes that "breathe." Natural fibers tend to look smarter. Above all, remember clothes that are cared for look smarter than those that are neglected—and at minimal extra cost.

SUCCESS AND SELF-ESTEEM

Shining success
Polishing up your sense of self-esteem will enhance every aspect of your life.

ONE OF THE BIGGEST advantages anyone can have in life is a strong and secure feeling of self-esteem—a respect for yourself and your worth as a person. When this is absent, no amount of material or worldly success can, by itself, fill the gap.

Although self-esteem inspires confidence, the outward appearance of confidence is not the same thing as real self-esteem. This is partly because people whose overall self-image is extremely negative can still have confidence within a small area of expertise or skill: Those who are painfully shy in social situations, for example, often communicate fluently when the conversation turns to a topic in which they are passionately interested.

It's also true that many apparent signs of confidence, such as boasting and bullying, are more likely to indicate its absence; people with a healthy self-regard have no need for these tactics. Finally, many individuals whose self-esteem is low become adept at giving the impression of confidence.

In her book *Peoplemaking*, Virginia Satir refers to the family as a "factory." This analogy is extremely useful, since the nature of the adults we become is inevitably shaped by childhood experience. In an emotionally healthy family, children are not only given unconditional and unselfish love, they are also made to feel that they are inherently worthy of love, respect, and value simply as human beings. Because of this validation, they grow up with positive, secure feelings about themselves and their place in the world.

In contrast, low self-esteem can almost always be traced to an early assimilation—and acceptance—of messages from one or both parents that a child is clumsy, stupid, weak, or unattractive. These negative messages give birth to an inner voice that, in later life, constantly invalidates everything we think, say, and do. In some cases, it's possible to change the pattern by substituting a voice that is positive and encouraging. So, if you tend to approach challenges by telling yourself, "I know I'm going to fail," make a concentrated effort to change the message to "I know I can do this." An important lesson to absorb is that making a mistake, or failing in one area, does not have to invalidate how you feel as a whole person.

Change the pattern

Another idea is to alter any manageable behavior patterns that reinforce your low self-esteem. If excess weight is making you feel inadequate and unattractive, for example, sticking to a rigid diet may be too much to ask of yourself. Polishing off a whole box of chocolates, on the other hand, is guaranteed to fill you with self-disgust.

Even when weight is not an issue, regular exercise not only improves health and appearance. It can also build confidence by providing tangible proof of what you can accomplish when you try.

Such tactics can be extremely effective in breaking harmful patterns of thought and behavior. Remember, though, that where damage to self-esteem is serious and long-standing, psychotherapy or counseling may be the best way forward.

THE PEOPLE FACTORY

As a parent, perhaps the most important responsibility that you have is to nurture the self-esteem and self-image of your children. On the other hand, for many people this ego-boosting duty can be one of the most difficult, complex, and often bewildering aspects of parenting. For instance, if you happen to have a low self-esteem, which is due in part to your upbringing, then you might feel too inadequate or even incapable when it comes to instilling self-confidence in your own children. However, bearing in mind a few essential guidelines will aid you in helping your children to forge solid and well-rooted self-esteem.

• Listening carefully and attentively to what your children say as well as letting them know that you respect and honor their feelings and opinions, when practicable, are the most fundamental of these self-esteem guidelines.

• When the situation is appropriate, allow your children to express freely their fear, hurt, or anger without demanding that they "stop crying,"or "be brave."

• Let your children make small decisions for themselves; even choosing between a bunch of strawberries and a bunch of raspberries will help them learn how to exercise and develop their own judgment. Your children will then be less likely to rely on the evaluations of others or be pressured by their peers into doing things just because others are doing them.

• Treat your children with courtesy. For example, if due to lack of living space, your child's room must be vacated for a visitor, discuss the situation beforehand and explain how much you value his or her cooperation. Make sure that the child knows that you recognize the inconvenience that the temporary move is causing him or her. Also, say "please" and "thank you" to your child, and respect his or her possessions—if you want to borrow a book or toy, for instance, ask the child's permission first. In other words, show your child the same courtesy you would give others.

• Provide your children with plenty of affection and encouragement for all the things that they do. Keep in mind, though, that praise must be honest; children will sense when they have not done very well, so false praise will cause them to question their own instincts as well as your motivation. In most cases, it is better to acknowledge—but not dwell on—your children's failures, and instead give them genuine praise for all the effort that went into trying.

Check Your Self-Esteem

Everyone needs a healthy level of self-esteem to lead a full and happy life. How much self-esteem do you have? This quiz will help you discover which areas of your life you feel most positive and negative about. Rate each of these statements on a scale from one to five. If the statement does not apply to you at all, score one; if you agree completely, give yourself five. Then turn to "Solutions," on pages 140-141, to see how you score.

Career and work situations

1. I work very hard and conscientiously, and others consider that I am good at my job.
2. I am a person who tends to take the initiative and puts energy into making things happen.
3. I take change in my stride and respond to it positively, even when it is very challenging.
4. I do not feel threatened by the talent and ability of other people, whatever their achievements.
5. I always give praise to colleagues and subordinates when it is due.
6. I always try to learn something from my mistakes, whatever they are.
7. I am prepared to be adventurous in my career and take calculated risks to get ahead.
8. I am worth every penny of the salary I am paid.
9. I am honest in my professional dealings.
10. I have good and cooperative relationships with my colleagues.
11. I am not afraid of taking tough decisions.
12. I feel respected and valued by my immediate superiors and my company generally.

Social life and friendships

1. I consider myself an asset at a dinner or drinks party, and play a full part in any social gathering.
2. I enjoy meeting new people, learning about their lives and telling them about mine.
3. I am gregarious and sociable.
4. I can always find something appropriate, interesting or amusing to talk about.
5. I don't find it difficult to put shy or awkward people at their ease.
6. I am hospitable and love welcoming friends and relatives to my home.
7. I am broad-minded and enthusiastic with a wide and varied range of interests.
8. I have a good sense of humor and I enjoy the process of making other people laugh.
9. I seldom get bored and do not usually find it difficult to make the most of my free time.
10. I am able to trust and confide in a small group of close friends about everything important to me.
11. I feel comfortable expressing my feelings.
12. I am a good listener.

Character and personality

1. I have a warm and friendly personality.
2. I can accept constructive criticism without taking offence, and I try to learn from it.
3. I can stand up for myself, I am appropriately assertive, and I am able to say no when necessary.
4. I am fair, flexible, and open-minded in my views and attitudes about the world.
5. I avoid being judgmental in my opinions and reactions to other people.
6. I am a compassionate and humane person.
7. I try to be unselfish and generous in my dealings —business and otherwise—with other people.
8. I do not suffer from envy or jealousy.
9. I am not burdened with guilt.
10. I am not a vindictive person, and I don't hang on to resentment.
11. I am sensitive to the feelings of others.
12. I have an open and loving heart.

Physical appearance and health

1. Although I don't consider my appearance to be outstanding, I am happy with the way I look.
2. My weight is acceptable for my age and height.
3. My face is attractive, and my normal expression is relaxed and friendly.
4. I have a pleasing figure and consider myself sexually attractive.
5. I feel comfortable with my body.
6. I take responsibility for my health and I eat a well-balanced diet.
7. I rarely get drunk and only ever drink alcohol in strict moderation.
8. The amount of cigarettes I smoke is not likely to affect my health.
9. I make sure that regular exercise is an important part of my daily routine.
10. I make the effort to look good for my own sake as much as for others.
11. I accept small imperfections and wouldn't want to eradicate them with plastic surgery.
12. I do not believe that someone has to be young to be considered beautiful.

JUGGLING RESPONSIBILITIES

THESE DAYS, WORKING PEOPLE often find it difficult to find a healthy balance in their lives between family and career. At its best, combining a happy family life with a successful career is enormously fulfilling, but making this arrangement work on a day-to-day level, and constantly juggling a number of conflicting responsibilities, can feel like an impossible task.

Career versus children?

The days are long gone when the only career open to women was that of "housewife." Traditionally women were expected to have children and look after the home while their husbands bore total financial responsibility for the family. For many women—and an increasing number of men—combining family life and childcare with a fulfilling career that is not centered around the home has become the norm. Accomplishing this, however, takes patience, and considerable organization.

Jobs and children, for instance, both require a great deal of commitment, and their needs can often be conflicting; most full-time jobs require employees to be at work during specified hours, usually around 9 to 5, but the school day is shorter than this. What's more, school holidays are weeks or months longer than even a generous holiday entitlement. One option is paid childcare, but this can be extremely hard to find, as well as more expensive than many parents are able to afford.

It is not just women who feel torn about where their priorities lie. Men tend to work longer hours than women, particularly when their children are small, simply because it is at this stage that they are establishing their career momentum, or laying the foundations of a business. Also, many working women choose to stay at home during their children's first few years, so they need the extra money that working long hours generates, even though they would infinitely prefer their partner to spend more time at home. This situation can produce enormous conflict—while a father knows that his first priority is his family, he may have to neglect them occasionally when the demands of his job become overwhelming. Make sure, though, that these absences do not become the norm, since long-term neglect can damage a parent/child relationship irrevocably.

Whatever form your struggle takes, one vital rule is to avoid trying to be superman or superwoman. Becoming hooked on "having it all," and being all things to all people, can stop you from enjoying—or even coping with—your life.

Lucy, for example, had three children under the age of ten, and a solid relationship with her husband, Max. She also had a very demanding job as a financial manager in a large corporation. The whole family had a number of interests that they pursued, both together and separately, and on the surface their lives seemed very happy. Lucy, however, had begun to feel that she was on a treadmill: as soon as she took the children to school, she was on the car phone talking to clients. After a demanding day at the office, she went home to link up with the nanny, put the children to bed, prepare an elaborate meal, clean the house, and cope with the family laundry. In addition, she was the secretary of her local parent/teacher association. As a result, Lucy was constantly exhausted, and she never had a moment to relax, to see her friends, or to explore any of her own interests.

First things first

Eventually, Lucy realized that things had to change. She arranged with her husband that he would take on more household chores, and she accepted that eating simpler meals, including the occasional takeaway, would do her family no harm. She resigned her PTA duties, and paid someone else to take care of the cleaning and ironing. One evening a week, Max looked after the children so Lucy could go out. Taking these steps enabled her to regain her spirits, revive her old friendships, and recharge her batteries.

Part-time work

Statistics indicate that in most families, women—even those with careers outside the household—still bear primary responsibility for childcare: when a child is sick, for example, the mother is more likely than the father to take time off work. One of the ways many working mothers cope with the responsibility is by taking a part-time job, yet the part-time work traditionally available to women is often badly paid, or menial, or both. Due to the need for flexibility in an unstable economic climate, however, and the dramatic advances in telecommunications technology, this pattern is changing, and part-time work is now the fastest growing sector of the employment market. So, even if previous attempts to explore this solution to your dilemma have been unsuccessful, another try might bear fruit.

Another effective tactic is self-employment, and many women set up businesses that can be run from home during the school day. Two mothers could even share this responsibility if one looks after all the children while the other runs the business, and vice versa. Some resourceful women even turn the problem into a solution by setting up a nursery to provide care for their own children as well as those of other working parents.

Making It Work

In the face of conflicting demands of job and family, many parents recognize that something has to give and they have to reach a compromise. The following tips will help you to limit the stress of trying to juggle your responsibilities.

- Delegate whatever you can—don't try to do everything yourself.
- Employ someone else for domestic chores such as housework and car-washing.
- Organize an efficient back-up strategy so that if your usual childcare arrangements fall through at short notice, your work will not suffer dramatically.
- Although your life needs to be well organized, it's also important that you allow yourself some unstructured time for relaxation and enjoyment.
- Recognize that it's seldom possible to accomplish everything, or always be the best. Be realistic and learn to live with imperfection and compromise.

NEW WAYS OF WORKING

As the twentieth century draws to a close, more and more people are changing their patterns of work. In the past, a person would have one employer and one line of work for their entire professional lives. Nowadays, due to the rapid advances in computers and communication technology, and the changing demands of both employers and employees, it seems it will become increasingly rare for a person to remain with one company for life.

The new workplace

Very many people are now working in non-traditional ways. Short-term contracts are becoming more popular as a way of reducing long-term staff costs; computers, fax machines, and modems are enabling people to work at home and send their work back to base; increasing numbers of people are self-employed or freelance, and others have a number of part-time jobs which add up to more than a full-time job's hours. More and more people working like this will have to be responsible for their own taxes, pensions, training, sick pay, and unemployment insurance—all things traditionally looked after by employers or the state.

How you feel about these changes will probably be influenced by whether or not you have chosen them or had them forced upon you. Some people decide to become self-employed or work at home because they have easily marketable skills and want the freedom to expand and work how and when they choose. They are thus likely to be much happier than people who have to work on short-term contracts because that is all the work that is available.

If, however, your work situation is not of your choosing, you can still make the choice to be positive about it, and make sure that you use all your contacts in order to maximize your chances of success. It is worth remembering that while having a "job for life" offered security, it often stifled people's initiative, and made their lives predictable, not always allowing them to achieve their potential.

Management theorist Charles Handy, in his books *The Age of Unreason* and *The Empty Raincoat,* argues that in the future people will have "portfolio careers,"

Keep it separate
When you work at home, it can be hard to keep the two areas of your life separate. You will be most successful, however, when you find some way of knowing how and when work ends and leisure time begins.

where they have a range of experience and a variety of skills that they can sell to those who may want them. This has the distinct advantage that if you do not have one "job," but a variety of ways to earn your living, then the loss of one source of income is not a disaster—you can always turn to the others.

Working at home

There are many advantages to working at home—the freedom to decide when you clock on and off, the lack of commuting, fewer distractions—but there is also a downside. If you are planning to work at home, it is important to be aware of the disadvantages, so you can find strategies to avoid them.

The most obvious disadvantage is that there is a lack of boundary between work and home, so that the one spills into the other. This can mean you rarely stop working, and that a fax arriving from someone in another time zone can wake the whole family. At the very least, try to have a separate room as an office, rather than working at the kitchen table. Perhaps an office could be set up in the garden shed, so that you would know when you were going "out" to work, and when you were leaving for the day.

Another disadvantage of working at home is isolation. This can be tackled by making yourself go out at lunchtime, perhaps to the swimming pool, or for a walk in the park. Alternatively, arrange one day of meetings a week away from home, or try and do work in your clients' offices from time to time. This can also help you gain the stimulation that comes from discussing ideas with other people.

Fluctuating work patterns—too much one week, nothing the next—should be tackled by having other, stable interests that you are committed to outside work. Although your job might not be perfect, having a well-rounded life will help you to place work in a healthier perspective.

New men

Now that men are no longer necessarily the chief breadwinners in a family, new opportunities are opening up for them to choose how they want to organize their time. Not all men have been satisfied with being marginalized from their children's lives because they were working so hard. Some are now opting to work fewer hours so that they can take a fuller part in childcare. They are coming to realize that spending time with their children offers emotional rewards not on offer in the world of work.

Others are working fewer hours so that they can improve the quality of their lives in other ways. Sam, for example, had always wanted to return to higher education and study for a masters degree. His children had grown up, and his wife had a career of her own. When he was made redundant, he decided that he had to make the choice between finding another job and doing what he had always wanted, so he enrolled in college. Using his previous work skills, he managed to gain consultancy work for several days a week, which allowed him time for his academic work—as well as earning more money than he had received for his previous full-time work.

Sam found that he enjoyed the freedom this new way of working offered him. When he finished his degree, he decided to continue pursuing his consultancy work, as well as devoting more time to his grandchildren. That way, he really felt he was getting the best of both worlds.

OVERCOMING OBSTACLES

THE ROAD TO SUCCESS is littered with practical problems that have to be overcome before you can do the things you want. Many of these problems, such as discrimination and harassment, are created by others; some, like parenthood, are the consequence of your own life choices. Nevertheless, with careful planning these obstacles can often be overcome, or at least challenged so their effects are minimized.

Prejudice and discrimination

People in all walks of life find themselves up against prejudice and discrimination, which can be formidable obstacles preventing them from getting what they want. Being denied employment or advancement because you are the "wrong" race, gender, age, sexuality, or because you are disabled is unfair and insulting. Although these days there is more recognition by some large companies that discrimination is counterproductive—because it results in so much skill, knowledge, and wisdom going to waste—far too many people are still overlooked.

In many countries, legislation exists to combat some types of prejudice, and if you think you have been a victim of it, you should take legal advice. However, other forms of prejudice, such as ageism, are rampant and largely unchallenged—so much so that people over the age of 40 who are made redundant generally find it hard, often impossible, to get a job interview, much less a job. If you are being discriminated against, do not just sit back and take it, as that way you'll become a victim. Instead, gain inspiration from all the people

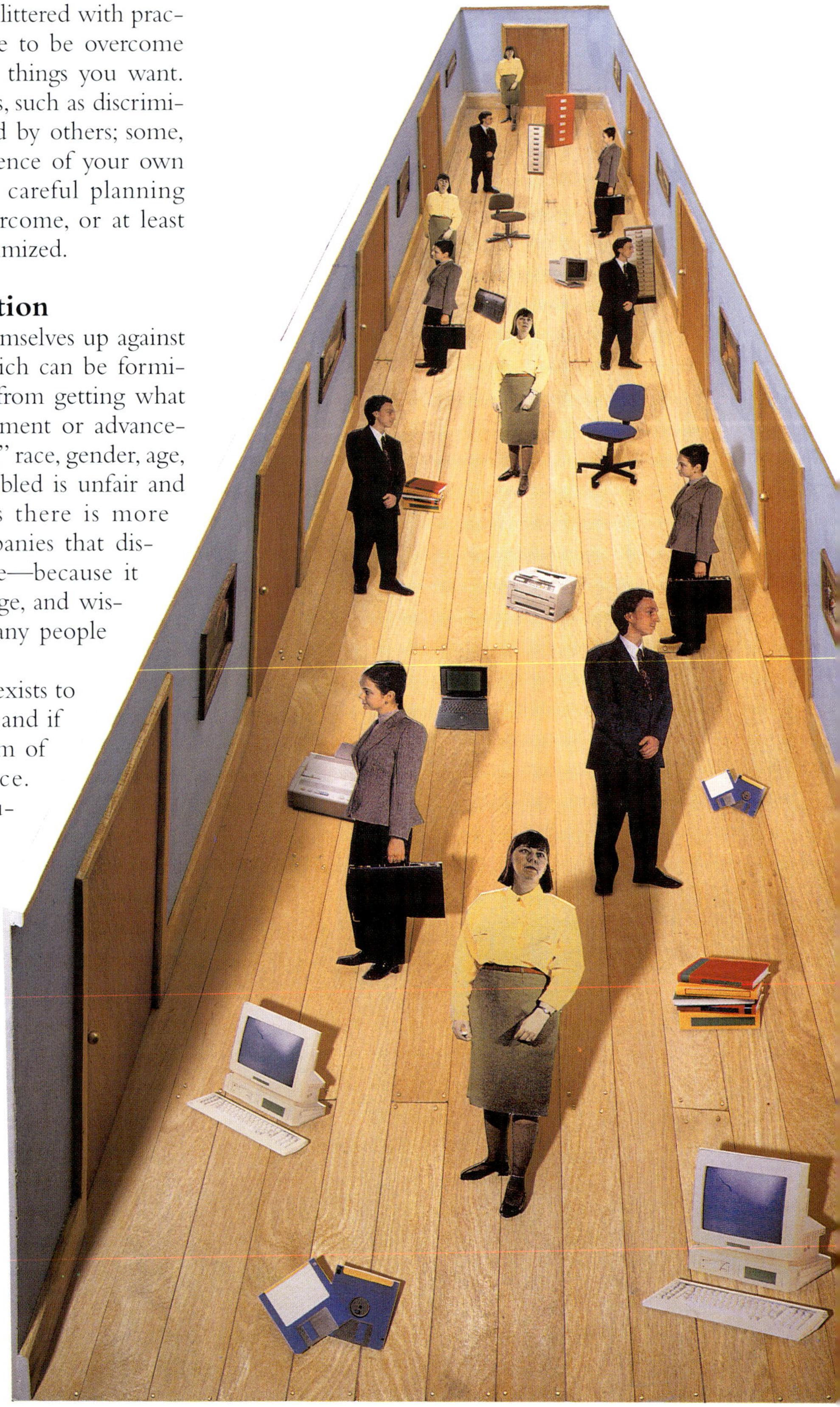

An obstacle course

Whether you have to move around them, go through them, or climb over them, workplace obstacles must be negotiated if you are to succeed.

in your position who have succeeded, and see what they have done—perhaps you might think of setting up in business on your own, or with a group of people in a similar situation.

Sexual harassment

Although sexual harassment affects both sexes, the majority of victims are women. It can be one of the most upsetting and humiliating experiences imaginable, affecting confidence and the ability to function. In practice, you are being sexually harassed if someone makes you the target of any unwelcome sexual attention. This includes having lewd, suggestive remarks made to you, being shown sexually oriented pictures, or being touched in a sexual way. It is also sexual harassment if someone insults or ridicules you because of your sex, or makes it known that your career will be affected by whether or not you are prepared to give sexual favors.

In her book *Making Advances*, Liz Curtis sets out the following step-by-step procedure for dealing with unwanted sexual harassment:

- Inform the harasser that the behavior is unacceptable and must end. If you do this in writing, keep a copy of the letter; if you prefer personal confrontation, ask someone in a senior position to be a witness.
- Note the date and time of each incident, with details of what happened.
- Report the harasser to someone in authority. Even if nothing is done, this step is important for any legal action.
- If you are touched on an intimate part of your body, report the harasser to the police for indecent assault.
- If no one in your company is helpful, contact an outside agency, such as a law center or a women's organization.

Many of these problems are difficult ones, and constant battles can take their toll on all aspects of your life. So be very clear that, although it is your responsibility to do what you can, the original situation is not your fault. Remember, too, that other people have triumphed and achieved success in different ways, despite all of the many obstacles which have been put in their paths.

CARING FOR CHILDREN

For many women, the lack of suitable childcare is a serious obstacle to achieving at work. Indeed, a recent report showed that a sizable number of women doctors in Britain have given up practicing medicine because they cannot find part-time work that would enable them to combine their professional and family commitments.

For the majority of working women, becoming mothers means they are regarded as less efficient, regardless of evidence to the contrary. A few companies are now opening up so-called "windows of opportunity" in the form of jobshares, flexible hours, and workplace nurseries. Far too many, however, still take no account of the demands of children, such as parents' days, sudden illness, or the breakdown of childcare arrangements.

Some women cope by setting their own terms of employment. Jenny, a senior television executive, has successfully combined motherhood with a high-powered and pressurized job. At her interview for the editorship of a daily current affairs program, she set out her terms. "When I said during my interview that I must be able to accompany my children to and from school once a week, a sort of silence fell... Afterwards everyone said I'd probably spoiled any chance I had of getting the job." Fortunately Jenny's abilities were so highly regarded that her bosses gave her both the job and the domestic concession.

What this example illustrates is that if you are highly sought after for a position, you can get help. So ask for what you want—if you don't ask, you won't get it.

THE GLASS CEILING

The glass ceiling is a phenomenon about which many women in the workplace know all too well—they achieve a certain level, they can see where they want to go, but an "invisible" barrier keeps preventing them from making further progress. In what is now referred to as the post-feminist era, women everywhere are still having difficulty achieving basic equality with their male colleagues at work.

That old, familiar story

Sandra Davis, a marketing consultant, started work during the 1980s for a recruitment agency whose board of directors was made up entirely of men. She knew that it would be hard to get on the board, but she was confident that her ability and ambition would eventually win out. Eight years, and several promotions later, however, she had to face the sad fact that she would never get to board level.

The hard truth was that Sandra had been promoted as far as her superiors were prepared to let her go. Looking back over her time there, she said she felt that there were a million subtle ways in which she was never taken quite seriously enough, never given full credit or respect for what she had done. In the end, she chose to leave and set up her own business.

What Sandra experienced is happening every day in the vast majority of work situations. To be successful, women often feel they have to be twice as good as men, and battle every step of the way along their career path; then, at the end of the day, they find themselves cheated of their ultimate goal.

Through the glass ceiling

" 'Let's pretend the glass has gone all soft like gauze, so that we can get through,' said Alice." This quote from *Through the Looking Glass* is cited by Carole McKenzie in her own book, *Presenting for Women in Business*. Like many, she feels that, if women adjust their mental outlook, they can achieve a great deal. Many others share her view. Nancy Kline, a consultant in women's leadership development and author of *Women and Power: How Far Can We Go?*, acknowledges that shattering the glass ceiling may well involve "a level of confidence and a sense of self-worth that, trapped inside our conditioned desire to defer and promote others, we find terrifying."

However, there are certain formidable strategies that women can develop to ease their progress. These new strategies will help you to gain more control over your working life in general:

• Work on developing a sense of self-belief—assertiveness training classes have helped countless women to discover new strength and confidence.

• Look for the best opportunities on offer—and take them up. Don't simply complain that your ideal opportunity hasn't appeared yet.

• Be prepared to widen your career horizons—too many women have been brought up with very narrow ideas about possible career paths; now is the time

to find out more and perhaps throw up some options you have never considered before.

- Study to obtain the necessary skills and qualifications.
- Want to succeed badly enough, and have enough determination, to make your dreams a reality.
- If you are a working mother, try not to let guilt swamp your ambitions. This is very hard, but don't feel that you have to manage everything alone. Press partners, friends, and relatives into service so that you can arrive at a comfortable home/work split.

On their own terms

Many people believe that, to be successful, a woman must imitate a man. This attitude, however, is increasingly rejected by today's working women, who want to be successful without sacrificing their feminine qualities. Nancy Kline maintains that women who submit to the dehumanizing aspects of corporate power are those still subscribing to the idea that successful women have to operate in a masculine way.

It may be that this is not only untrue but actually counterproductive, emphasizing some of the worst aspects of business. A former Businesswoman of the Year says, "I hate the power games men play. I have always thought it was wrong to ask women to change themselves. That way, they become one of the boys and bring nothing new to their job." The world of business, however, can only gain from the special qualities women have to offer—qualities such as compassion, perceptiveness, and intuition.

Breaking Through

If you encounter a glass ceiling, how will you deal with it? Will you shatter the glass with a bold strategy, or behave as though it were gauze and adopt a more subtle, kid-gloved approach? Your choice will depend on your personality and the situation in question.

Shattering the glass

For example, Cheryl had reached the position of art director at her advertising company when one of its directors left. Cheryl felt that she was his obvious successor, but knew that no woman had ever been a director there before. She arranged a meeting with the chairman, pointing out that her campaigns had made the company greater profits than ever before. He said that he would consider her appointment.

A week later she hadn't heard anything so she arranged another meeting. Her boss admitted having reservations, although he wouldn't say exactly what these were. Cheryl reminded him that if she left, her clients might well go, too. Could he afford to lose both her and the clients? The next day she got the promotion.

Tearing the gauze

Dawn had been with the same publishing company for five years. She had joined as a managing editor—having forged an impressive reputation at her previous job—and had been promised swift promotion. After a couple of years, however, she had been passed over for the position of publisher several times. She determined to do all that she could to get the job she felt she deserved.

The first thing Dawn did was to adjust her attitude to a positive one, so that she did not start to feel that her gender was automatically a problem. She approached her ultimate goal as a long-term project, drawing up a series of sub-goals. After arranging several lunches with the company president, Dawn was given more responsibility. She quickly showed a growing knowledge about the general workings of the business, and the president showed his appreciation by giving her pay rises at every opportunity. When the company's publisher retired, Dawn pointed out the qualities that she could bring to the post. The president agreed.

NETWORKING

The art of making and using contacts—also known as networking—is a useful, and potentially very successful, way of opening up business or career opportunities that you might otherwise never get to hear about.

A common misconception about networking is that it only involves people who are already influential and in positions of power. Of course, people in this situation do use their contacts—the "old boys' network," for example, refers to former pupils of the same small group of private schools or universities who appoint each other to top jobs and positions of power. But everyone knows people—from friends, relatives, and ex-colleagues to members of the same trades union or professional body—who can help them succeed.

The advantages of networking

Networking can be a very effective way of gaining information, finding out about jobs, and knowing what is happening right now in a particular field. For instance, you may want to move from teaching to a job in management. By expressing an interest in management to friends, family, acquaintances, neighbors, and anyone you meet, you will probably find someone who has information you can use.

How to network

According to Cynthia Chin-Lee, author of *It's Who You Know*, chatting to the most unlikely people can yield results. Even if you don't find it easy to start a conversation with strangers, she suggests disclosing a little about yourself at every opportunity. After a new contact has advised you, particularly if they have done you a favor, she advises always writing a thank-you note, which reinforces your relationship.

Rosemary, for example, was a successful photographic stylist until she married and moved to the

Giving each other a helping hand
Even if you don't think you're well connected, you are bound to know some people who can help you. From family members to people you meet at parties, the most unexpected people may be able to direct you toward new opportunities.

States. Ten years later she left her husband and returned to Europe. She found that her professional world had changed significantly during her absence and realized it would not be easy to re-establish herself. Her route back into work was via networking. She renewed contacts with people she had worked with and enlisted the help of friends, family, and anyone else she met. Ex-colleagues referred her to new people and so her network expanded. After three months this informal networking paid off. She was invited to a book launch, where she bumped into a photographer she had known twenty years before. He ran a photo library and was looking for an assistant. Rosemary was just the sort of person he wanted, so he offered her the job.

Networking is not a magic solution to career problems—it can only complement the skills, experience, and creativity that you already have. Even if you get a job because of "who you know," it is only your expertise that will help you keep it. But good contacts, used well, can kick-start your career.

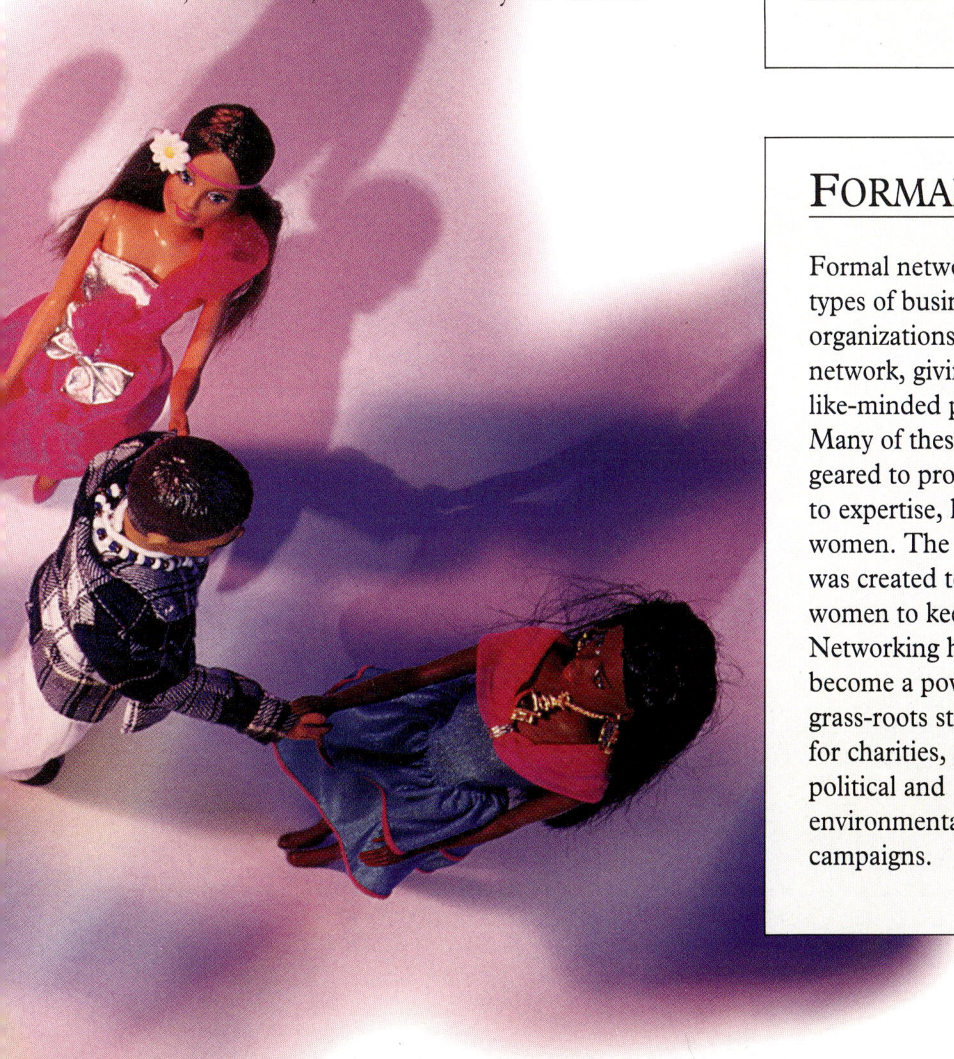

Informal Networking

Informal networking is straightforward. It is a matter of keeping a contact book in which you list the names, addresses, and phone numbers of all the people you know. Beside each name make a note of what they do and how you think they may be able to help you, and, where possible, how you might help them. Make your list as long as possible. Include school and college friends, friend's husbands or wives, friends of friends, and people you met at parties. Keep in contact by seeing people for lunch, for example, or organizing dinner parties. The object is to build relationships that are mutually advantageous and direct.

Formal Networking

Formal networks are centered around certain types of businesses or occupations. These organizations fill the gaps in your personal network, giving you the opportunity to mix with like-minded people working in the same field. Many of these formal networks, which are usually geared to promoting self-help and can offer access to expertise, have been formed by women, for women. The *City Women's Network*, for example, was created to allow professional women to keep in touch. Networking has also become a powerful grass-roots strategy for charities, and political and environmental campaigns.

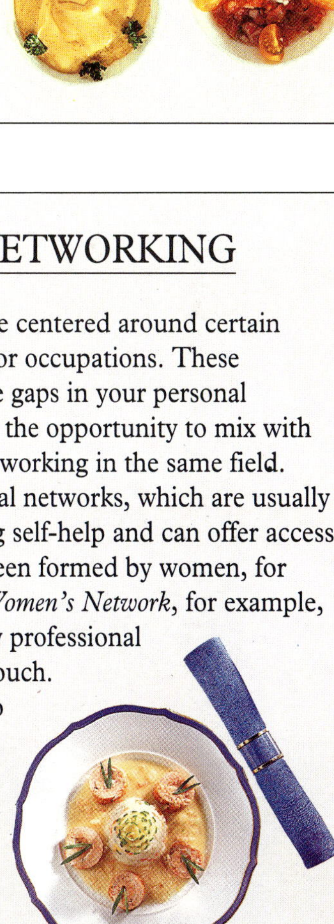

507NK

CHAPTER FOUR

COPING WITH SUCCESS

SUCCESS IS NOT AN END in itself. As soon as you achieve success you need to work to keep it. For example, if promotion at work is your goal, once you are promoted you will find you need to continue to work hard to prove yourself worthy of, and successful in, your new position. Ultimately, perhaps, you will want to work toward further promotion—and so the process continues.

Furthermore, although you may achieve success in one area of your life, other areas—your home life, your social life, even your health—may suffer as a consequence (see "Don't Overdo It," pp. 114-115) and need to be worked at even harder. A truly successful life is a well-balanced life, and should include vacations, time for relaxation, for friends, and for activities that are completely unrelated to your work. This may seem an impossible dream, but it is actually just a question of making the right decisions. You cannot ignore any elements of your life, because if you do a problem may arise to cast a shadow over your achievement.

All this may leave you with the impression that success is only attainable by a few super-humans. Of course this is not the case, it is simply that there are traps that are easy to fall into, such as being overwhelmed by stress or becoming addicted to work (see "Are You a Workaholic?" pp. 116-117). The purpose of this chapter is to show you how to handle these crises. Moreover, challenges or setbacks should not be seen as failures but opportunities for experience and valuable tests of your abilities.

This chapter will also help you to address the emotional challenge of success. A mixture of emotions—such as fear, guilt, pride, enjoyment, anxiety, and insecurity—often accompanies achievement. This can be very destructive and leave you feeling confused. It is therefore important to be aware of how your emotional response to success may affect your behavior. In particular, beware of becoming arrogant, vain, ruthless, or patronizing. You must also be sensitive to the fact that your success is likely to arouse envy in others.

But most important of all, this chapter shows you that it's never too late to set your sights on success. It is possible to overcome your fears about change (see pp. 128-129), and take steps to prepare yourself for whatever lies ahead in order to make it more manageable. Being able to cope with all these challenges is, in fact, the ultimate proof of your success.

ANY SUCCESS WORTH HAVING WILL NOT BE EASY TO ACHIEVE. THE MEASURE OF YOUR SUCCESS WILL, IN FACT, REFLECT HOW YOU COPE WITH THE PROBLEMS AND SETBACKS YOU MEET ALONG THE WAY.

FACING PROBLEMS

"EXPERIENCE IS THE NAME every man gives to his mistakes." So said Oscar Wilde, the famous nineteenth-century writer and wit. No one goes through life without making mistakes and encountering problems; what distinguishes a successful person is how they deal with these experiences and what they learn from them. Every time you tackle a problem with a positive mental attitude, you become a stronger person, more able to make the most out of life's disappointments. Now is the time to start thinking about the most effective kinds of positive strategies to overcome any difficulties in your life.

A golden opportunity

It is through coping with problems that we really come face to face with ourselves. Try to think of difficult situations as giving you the chance to learn something about yourself—your strengths as well as your weaknesses and fears. Perhaps, for example, it has become a huge problem for you to cope with a responsible position at work, and yet you feel unfulfilled in a work role where you have little control. Are your fears of responsibility fed by limiting self-beliefs—you are convinced that you are simply not capable/clever/well-qualified enough to take a higher position? Limited self-beliefs can become a destructive straightjacket, causing all kinds of problems and then stopping you from dealing with them.

Coping with the setbacks

If you don't manage to deal with a challenging or problematic situation to your satisfaction, there is always the danger that this setback will cause you to go out of your way to avoid similar situations in the future. By doing this, you could well be shutting yourself off from potentially fulfilling situations and opportunities of all kinds.

Bearing the following points in mind will help you to make the most of life's inevitable setbacks:

- Don't waste time and energy brooding on your setback. Always look forward rather than backward.
- In any given scenario, learn from your mistakes while keeping your main objectives in view—"failure" may be hard to accept, but it does not mean giving up your goals. Look at the experience closely. You will probably discover that there was nothing wrong with your goal—it was the approach that was wrong. Stop saying "I'll never do that again" after a setback. Instead, try, "I'll never do it *like that* again."

Positive thinking in action

Joanna wanted to start her own business, and made an appointment to see her bank manager about financial assistance. Despite feeling that she had prepared well for the interview, she did not make a good impression. The bank manager adopted a rather condescending tone and finally turned her down. Joanna was both angry and upset—mainly with herself, for failing to make a good impression.

The next day, having calmed down a little, she reviewed the meeting as honestly as she could. She began to see that, although she was well prepared on paper, with a well-thought out business plan and a list of possible questions and answers, she had not yet worked out how to deal assertively enough with the bank manager's patronizing manner.

She decided to try another bank. Before going to see the manager there, she asked a friend to give her a mock interview. By redirecting her strong feelings of anger and frustration—due to her last setback—into a determination to succeed, she found it much easier to adopt a positive, assertive manner. This time around, Joanna was successful in securing her loan. What she had decided to do was to examine her failed attempt in order to pinpoint her weak area, and then address this constructively, rather than simply condemning herself across the board.

Putting yourself in perspective

A sense of perspective is all-important in dealing with problems and setbacks.

- Don't allow your general perception to be colored by one bad incident. Richard Bandler, in his book *Using Your Brain for a Change*, recounts the story of a woman who had been having a wonderful time at a party—until she spilled wine on her dress. Suddenly, her whole evening was ruined. All she saw was her stained dress. A more positive perception of the evening would be of a highly enjoyable occasion marred by one small accident.
- When confronted with a problem, try recalling times when tricky situations had unexpectedly positive outcomes—you might like to use visualization techniques for this (see "Creative Visualization," pp. 34-37). Also, think of all the people who have been through appalling happenings, and yet still value the experience as a chance to learn something about life and human nature.
- If you are in the midst of a crisis and find it hard to believe it will ever end, "reframe" the event so it does not dominate your life. Visualize yourself literally rising above it—standing on the moon, for example. Or imagine how your problem fits into the grand scheme of things by placing it in a historical context—or in the context of your whole existence.

So the important thing is to learn that the key is as follows—get things into perspective, learn from your "mistakes"—and then after that forget about them and get on with the rest of your life.

Aiming to win

If possible, deal with what you see as failure in a positive, even slightly playful, way. You can't score goals all the time, and no experience is a wasted one that should simply be thrown away.

Don't Overdo It

YOU WON'T BE truly successful if you don't know when you are overdoing it. There is, after all, no point in being rich and "having it all" if your life is made a misery due to overwork and excessive stress. A degree of stress, however, is not a bad thing. If you experience it as mild pressure or challenge, it can stimulate you and actually improve your performance. Yet, when stress becomes too great and you are unable to cope with it, you may fall prey to a range of physical and psychological symptoms.

This job's killing me!

Some jobs seem to have stress built into them; others become stressful, as, for example, when an industry undergoes decline and jobs are at risk. A new boss, new technology, changes to existing working habits and relationships all have an effect. Change itself causes stress; then, as workers adapt, stress declines. Some bosses cause stress through poor management—last-minute decisions, failure to communicate information, and inconsistent discipline only serve to undermine others' confidence.

The precise point at which anyone will succumb to the effects of stress will vary according to personality type, support systems, and the number of stressful events that occur together. Because stress is cumulative, an individual may cope with a very busy and stressful job with comparative ease. However, when other stressful events occur, for example, the death of a close family relative or the birth of a new baby, the strain may be too much to bear. Alternatively, it can be a very small event, not stressful on its own, that proves the last straw.

Stress overload!
When you are overworked and highly stressed look out for your body's warning signals telling you to slow down.

What's Your Stress Level?

To assess the extent of job-related stress to which you are subjected, answer Yes or No to the following questions. Try doing the quiz at a time when you are highly stressed, then when you are feeling relatively calm, and compare the results.

1. Do you work to very tight and often unrealistic deadlines?
2. Do you work long hours?
3. Is the pace of your work determined by others, so that you are unable to plan your work?
4. Do you have too much to do? Or too little?
5. Are the requirements of your job unclear?
6. Are you at the beck and call of a number of different people, all with different expectations?
7. Do you believe your job to be insecure?
8. Does your workplace lack friendship/support systems?
9. Does your job involve dealing with other people's strong emotions (such as a doctor dealing with severe illness and death)?
10. Do you have little control over your own work and the way it is assessed?
11. Is your workplace very competitive?
12. Are you in the process of major change at work (for example, new technology, new boss, new job)?
13. Do you feel like a round peg in a square hole?
14. Do you dislike working for your boss?
15. Are you unable to get clear and helpful feedback?
16. Do you often say "Yes" at work when you would rather say "No?"
17. Does your boss make decisions that affect you without consulting you?
18. Does your job involve stressful and/or dangerous situations, such as those faced by police officers, news camera crews, or staff working in hospital emergency rooms?
19. Are you in a minority at work (for instance, a woman in a man's world)?
20. Have you just joined, just returned to, or are you about to leave your present employment?

Assessing your answers

The more often you answered Yes to a question the more stressful your work. This does not mean that you will necessarily suffer symptoms of stress, since you may have excellent stress-management skills, but the potential for problems is there.

If you answered Yes to 14 or more of these questions, your job is taking too big a toll. You should consider new ways in which you can cope.

How to deal with it

• Get a life! Make sure your priorities are clear. Learn to relax. Make sure that you have full and satisfying personal relationships and active leisure pursuits outside of work; this will help you to cope with your job (see "Raise Your Energy Levels," pp. 120-121).
• Build up support networks. "A problem shared is a problem halved," the old saying goes. Get together with your colleagues to share experiences at work and offer support to find viable solutions.
• Manage your job. Look at your work and consider ways in which you can exercise some control. If you would like more feedback on your work, could you approach your boss and ask for it? If there are too many conflicting demands on you, is there a way of simplifying things? This may involve you standing up to your boss—which will lessen your stress in the long run. Or, if too little time is your problem, perhaps you could go on a time management course.
• Stand up for yourself. If other people are giving you stress, handle them calmly and assertively. They may even respond positively to a more assertive approach.

Get organized!
It is worth spending time getting things organized. You will then find it much easier to step into the right pair of shoes for each of the many roles in your life.

ARE YOU A WORKAHOLIC?

If rushing around and being constantly busy seems to be taking over your life, you will not be able to enjoy your successes. Although many people have jokingly described themselves as "workaholic"—addiction to work being perceived as the most acceptable of addictions—it can be just as bad for your health and psychological well-being as other addictions.

Recognizing the signs

Work addiction can be compared with drug and alcohol addiction in many of its symptoms. Work addicts show typical characteristics of addictive behavior, such as compulsions and obsessions, persistence with the habit despite its negative effects, and denial that there is a problem.

One of the most obvious symptoms of workaholism is that work is having a negative effect on other parts of your life and on the people close to you. If accomplishing tasks is the only way you have of feeling good, you may well be addicted. Addiction to work shows itself in various ways and Diane Fassel, in her book *Working Ourselves to Death,* identifies four of them: the compulsive worker, the binge worker, the closet worker, and the work anorexic.

The compulsive worker

This is the stereotype of the workaholic and the most common form of work addiction. Compulsive workers work very long hours, take work home, work weekends, and are reluctant to take holidays. Such people are often perfectionists at work and unwilling to declare a piece of work complete. Compulsive workers often deny that the amount of work they do is of their own choice. They claim they are working for their family's sake, to maintain a certain lifestyle, or because the demands of their important and prestigious job make it essential. Sometimes, they promise those who are close to them that the period of intense

A balancing act

Workaholics often take on too much, piling one task on top of another. They run the risk that their work will become unmanageable.

working will soon be at an end. This is a false promise; one of the chief characteristics of compulsive workers is that as soon as one thing has been finished, it becomes essential to start on another.

The binge worker

Like the binge eater, the binge worker may go along at a normal pace for some time and then suddenly indulge in a frenetic burst of work. Like the binge drinker, the binge worker saves tasks up, and when things become difficult, submerges him or herself in work. Then he or she may go for days without sleep and become so focused on work that he or she loses all track of time. Bingeing may be difficult to detect since many of us have short periods of intense work; the binger is characterized by a constant pattern of work based on such episodes.

The closet worker

In public—where they can be observed—closet workers operate normally. However, secretly and unobserved, they put in a lot of additional work. The closet worker understands that there is something abnormal in their attitude to work and as a result may try to cut back on work under pressure from other people. However, he or she is seldom able to do so. In addition, some closet workers hide work by making it appear less than it is.

Diane Fassel quotes the case of Linda, the workaholic editor of a woman's magazine. In an attempt to reduce her weekend working hours, Linda promised her husband she would work on only three projects during Saturday and Sunday. This strategy worked for a few months and then the hours began to creep up again. She was still working on only three projects, but more and more work was being hidden under the three headings.

The work anorexic

A food anorexic's obsession with how much he or she eats leads to avoidance of food while thinking about it all the time. Similarly, the work anorexic thinks about work all the time but never does it. Such people feel that they can only work under intense pressure and procrastinate until the last minute. In an attempt to control work, they may commit themselves to punishing schedules to try to overcome a tendency to put things off.

Keeping it private
A closet workaholic will keep his or her addiction hidden from those who are closest. Although he or she might seem to work only normal hours, a closet workaholic will actually toil in secret.

How to change

Like other addictions, workaholism is often a way of not facing up to certain life problems or unresolved childhood issues. It takes courage to recognize what these might be and come to terms with them, but it is only by facing these problems that the underlying causes of addiction can be resolved. If you believe that you might be workaholic, then it is essential that you take steps to curb this addiction, perhaps by deciding to go on vacation and taking account of how much work is really appropriate. If you do not, then you will not be able to enjoy the success that you do achieve at work.

Take a Break

In order to be truly successful and fulfilled, you need to have a degree of balance in your life. There is little point in being incredibly successful at work if that is all you ever have time to do—as the old saying goes, "All work and no play makes Jack a dull boy." Any regular activity that interests you and is completely unrelated to your work life—it doesn't have to be a sport or something very creative—will enrich your enjoyment of life in general, and will almost certainly improve your performance at work.

Over the edge

When you lose a sense of balance in your life, work-related events can cause a major catastrophe. For example, John had a brilliant career as the commercial director of a transport company. His job entailed traveling all over the world striking deals, and working long hours when he returned to his office base. This lifestyle made it impossible for him to sustain a social life, or even make any new relationships. He had lost several serious girlfriends, moved away from his family, and drifted apart from old friends. He never took any time off for vacations and had no other interests—all he had the energy to do after he finished a day's work was to fall asleep in front of the television.

So, when his company was bought by a multinational, and he was laid off,

Walking a tightrope
Finding just the right balance for the different elements in your life—emphasizing leisure as much as work—will make you far happier and healthier.

John was shattered. He was paid off very handsomely, so earning money was not an urgent problem—but filling his time was. People told him to go away for a while and explore the world, but all John could think about was his overwhelming sense of failure, and getting another job as soon as humanly possible.

Discovering new priorities

Not working hit John so hard that he was forced to visit his local doctor for depression. The doctor recommended a counselor, who was able to help John view work in a more realistic light, and also helped him to explore other interests. Because all John's self-esteem and sense of identity had been bound up in his job, losing it made him feel that he was losing everything. It was six months before he got his next job, and in that time he began to learn that a more balanced way of life:

- promotes better health—both physical and mental
- is much more stimulating because it provides a greater degree of variety throughout your life
- gives you the opportunity to develop more satisfying human relationships

Making the change

There are countless people just like John, who find it impossible to give themselves a break. This is wrong—or it ought to be. If you are in a job where you are so indispensable that you cannot leave it for short periods, then the fault probably lies with your company. It may simply be demanding more from its staff than it is reasonable for them to give. It may be understaffed, or unwilling to train people so that tasks can be shared out evenly. Too few employers realize that, when people are overworked, they actually become less effective at their jobs.

Vacations are a vital part of enjoying life. On vacation, we recharge our batteries, spend time with friends and loved ones, explore different areas of the world, perhaps learn new skills—in fact, we live an entirely different life from the one we live day to day, and so can return to that life feeling enriched.

There is more to leisure time, however, than two weeks lying on a beach. Weekends away, courses where you learn new things just for the joy of learning, playing with your children, or cooking for friends, are all fun and rewarding. Work should be important and interesting—it should *not* be your life.

Leisure Goals

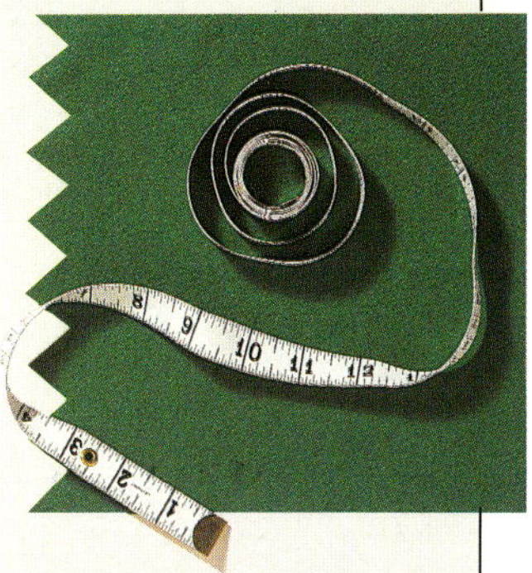

When you are planning your short- and long-term life goals, it is important to ensure that some of the things you want to do for fun and enjoyment go on your list. Take time to think about what it is that you would really like to do.

Perhaps you would like to design and make beautiful clothes for yourself. Do you need to go to classes, or can you teach yourself from a book? What equipment do you need? Which are the best fabric stores in your neighborhood? Or maybe you want to spend more time in the countryside. It's up to you to decide whether you would rather join a hiking group or simply go alone, to enjoy a peaceful closeness with nature.

One thing that holds many people back from making the most of their non-work hours is fear of loneliness. They may not go on vacation or join an evening class because they have no one to go with, and feel that doing such activities on their own would make them feel lonely. As a result they stay at home and feel even more lonely. Most people benefit from learning to be comfortable with their own company. If you alone can motivate yourself to undertake various activities, then you will have developed a great strength. Try telling someone close to you of your plans rather than musing about them to yourself—you will feel more impetus, and also more committed to carrying them out. But remember that staying at home doing nothing provides little stimulation, and little chance of meeting others. It is also easier to learn with the structure of a course, and the encouragement of a teacher and your fellow classmates.

Raise Your Energy Levels

However much you might want to be successful, and to get the most out of your life, your ability to either plan or act will be impaired if you feel tired all the time. And, if you do succeed in achieving your goals, lack of energy may mean that you don't have enough zest to enjoy your success to the full. You may think your lifestyle is too fraught to take steps toward improving your energy levels, but it is simpler to do this than you might think.

Fueling the machine

To keep your physical energy at a healthy level, you need to be careful about what you eat—advice that many people ignore. (See "How Healthy Is Your Life," p. 50.) The most important aspect of any diet is to eat well-balanced meals for the *majority* of the time. Any healthy eating regime must feature:

• Plenty of fresh fruit and vegetables, which are high in fiber, low in calories, and provide valuable vitamins and minerals. In theory, it should not be necessary to take vitamin supplements if you are eating a good balance of high-quality, fresh food. The vitamins, minerals, and trace elements particularly associated with energy are copper, iron, iodine, vitamin B12, and biotin (a B vitamin). These are found in liver, leafy green vegetables, nuts, and whole grains.

• Small, frequent meals, which maintain your energy levels and also keep you alert, rather than heavy, stodgy meals, which may put a strain on your digestive system, causing you to feel sleepy.

• Foods that provide a slow, steady energy supply, such as fruit, bread, and pasta. Those containing refined sugar may give you a quick lift when you are feeling tired, but this is followed by a quick drop in energy.

• Foods that won't over-stimulate your system. Caffeine, for example, will make you jittery and tense, even though you may be so used to drinking it that you no longer notice the effect. Instead, try peppermint tea for a healthier way to be alert. Also, you may be someone who finds that very highly spiced food makes your body feel over-stimulated and uncomfortable, so be on the look-out for this.

Exercising for energy

Regular, moderate exercise can help increase energy levels in several ways. Firstly, it works off the stress that accumulates in your daily life. Aerobic exercise—exercise that increases your pulse rate over a sustained period, such as swimming—speeds up the flow of oxygen around your body, increases the supply of oxygen to your lungs, and improves stamina. Research has shown that people who are physically fit perform better in tests of mental agility, and are more likely to be successful at whatever they set their sights on. Exercise need not take up a lot of time—20 minutes every other day will make a difference.

And so to sleep…

People vary a great deal in how much sleep they need. Find out the amount that is right for you, and try to ensure that it is as relaxed and untroubled as possible. If you have ever experienced insomnia, you will know how lack of sleep can

Charging your batteries
Regular exercise, the right amount of sleep, creative stimulation, and healthy eating are the batteries that will recharge your life.

destroy any energy for life—simply getting through the day becomes a strugle. In order to minimize the chances of insomnia:

- Take care to relax and unwind late in the evening, perhaps by listening to soothing music, having a milky drink or a peaceful bath.
- Try to take physical exercise at some point during the day, even if it is just a short brisk walk.
- Use a relaxation technique to help you if necessary (see "Taking Things Easy," right).

Energizing the mind

Everyone recognizes the feelings of mental exhaustion, when the pressures of work and daily life have pushed you to the extreme. In order to counteract this, it is helpful to have a creative outlet—a hobby that is as different as possible from what you do every day. If this can involve physical activity, so much the better: Gardening is one of the most popular leisure activities, and combines creativity with exercise. If you have a particularly stressful, challenging job, then it is probably a good idea to pursue leisure activities that are relaxing, and not competitive.

The best intentions

Most of us are aware of the things that we should be doing to raise our energy levels, and so enjoy a healthier existence, but it is always difficult to stick to good intentions; especially if we lead a busy life. Take things a step at a time. Perhaps start off by improving your eating habits and then move on to look at exercise and fitness. Set yourself small goals, for example, "Next time I'm going to swim five more lengths." But don't set yourself impossibly high standards. Remember, you want to increase your energy, not burn it out!

Taking Things Easy

In order to maintain your energy levels, it is essential that you make space in your schedule for relaxation—and without trying to do anything else at the same time. The following are easy and effective ways to relax:

Yoga classes always include relaxation techniques. For example: Lie on the floor, your arms and legs straight beside you and your palms turned upward. Breathe slowly and deeply, then, working upward from your toes, tense and relax every part of your body in turn.

Meditation can be very effective in counteracting stress. Sit very quietly, and imagine that you are sitting beside a river with the warm sun on your body. Imagine how you feel in that situation, and picture the look of the river, the feel of the grass beneath you, and the sun on your skin.

Aromatherapy is another useful aid to relaxation. Just before getting into a warm bath, add three drops of lavender oil and two of geranium oil, or three drops of sandalwood and one to two drops of marjoram oil. Do not use more than a total of ten drops of oil in a bath. Soak in the water for at least 20 minutes so that you will gain the full relaxing benefit.

Pamper yourself
Although you can't always avoid stressful situations, having regular times of relaxation will help you to cope better when stress arises.

HANDLING SUCCESS

IT WOULD SEEM THAT WE HAVE rather mixed feelings when it comes to success. Most people crave it, yet many suffer terrible physical and mental stresses when they actually achieve it. Success can have a wide range of effects—in the short term, some people panic or go to pieces; others develop a different personality, for either the better or the worse. And certain people finally feel free to do things they never had the confidence or energy to do before (see "Can You Handle Success?" p. 124).

Attitudes toward success

Our attitudes to successful people also vary—we can feel either glad or resentful, and this may depend on whether the "success" seems to be a matter of chance or the culmination of years of effort. When we hear about lottery winners whose lives have been ruined by petty squabbling, we may feel a degree of relief. Perhaps we want confirmation that success is bad for us—the success we don't have, that is!

Basically, the way you react to success depends very much on what it means to you. There are three main reasons why it may bring stress rather than enjoyment and pride: fear that you will be unable to maintain your success; guilt that you are unworthy of the success; and the shock of finding yourself in unfamiliar territory, with no bearings.

Fear of failure—or success?

One common anxiety to do with success is how to maintain it: when you feel that all eyes are focused on you, the pressures can be great. To succeed is to risk failure, and, as the saying goes, the higher you climb, the harder you fall. This is why many people feel increased anxiety when they have to live up to the reputation they have worked so hard to build. Such newly acquired fear—of failing after you have succeeded—may even be greater than the fear of never making it in the first place.

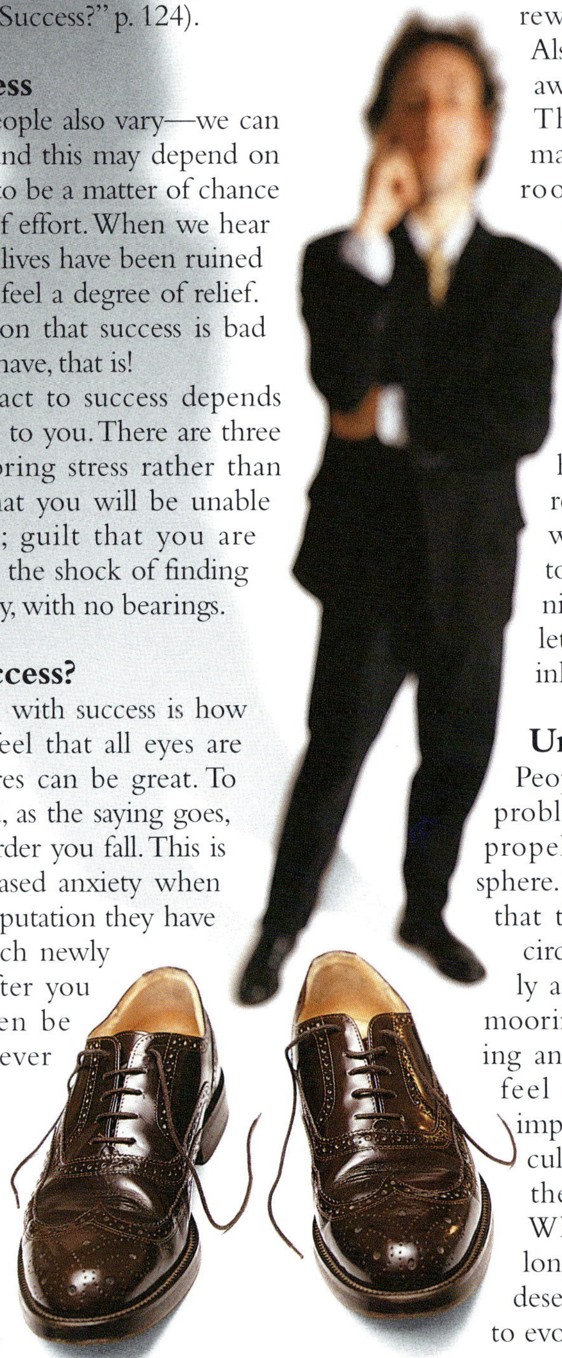

The shadow of success
A desire to remain an anonymous shadow may stop you stepping into more successful shoes.

Do I really deserve this?

Even if you have worked hard for your success, it is a common reaction to feel that you have succeeded purely by chance. Some people develop a terrible fear that they will be "found out" or thought to be undeserving. Usually this insecurity stems, not from reality, but from a conviction that, somehow, they don't deserve to succeed in any way. Such people find it hard to accept their success or enjoy the rewards that their success brings. Also, their difficulty can make life awkward for those around them. This kind of guilt, like fear of maintaining success, is frequently rooted in low self-esteem. You won't feel at ease with the new, successful you if you weren't happy with the original!

Guilt can also arise because we feel bad about receiving things—especially money—that more needy individuals don't have. For example, if we suddenly receive a windfall of some kind, we may give a generous donation to charity, or make an effort to be nicer to people in order to avoid letting anyone see the greed that is inherent in all of us.

Unfamiliar territory

People who succeed may encounter problems because their success has propelled them into another social sphere. Wealth or influence may mean that they find themselves mixing in circles that no longer include family and old friends. Adrift from their moorings, they may find life bewildering and frightening, especially if they feel obliged to put on an act to impress their new peers. These difficulties are more likely to crop up if the life change has been sudden. When you achieve success after long, hard work, you know that you deserve it, and your old life has time to evolve into a new one.

Case Histories

Haunted by success
Many people cannot deal with success, or the prospect of it, because they are haunted by guilt or fear.

Making others suffer

In many cases, successful people bring stress to others, rather than themselves. Everyone has met successful individuals who appear arrogant and insensitive. However, this may merely be the flip side of insecurity showing: for some people, success may offer their first taste of being "better" than others.

Take Paul, for example, who was painfully self-conscious as a boy. His sisters and brother always teased him, and he suspected that his father also considered him to be a failure. Paul grew into a shy, lonely teenager and young man, until he began working for someone who saw and fostered his potential. When Paul was eventually promoted, he changed into an arrogant person who rapidly became insensitive to the needs of others. This was his chance to do to others what had been done to him, and he did so, enjoying every minute. Eventually, Paul alienated everyone around him. Although he at last had the power that he had always longed for, he was once again alone and isolated.

Who, me?

Some people cope with success by denying that they have had anything to do with it. This may be due partly to a fear of arousing envy in others, or, in the case of Betty, because it may spoil their image. Betty was a quiet, shy woman known by her friends and colleagues as a very nice person, but definitely not as a dynamic achiever. Betty herself shared their views. When anything positive happened to her, she kept it secret. Although she did actually feel envious of anyone who was successful, being a loser meant that no one expected anything of her: it might not be much fun, but a loser can never suffer the pain of trying and failing.

Secret dreams

In his dreams, Alan was a rich, charismatic figure, respected by friends and colleagues and married to a beautiful, intelligent woman. In reality, he was a lonely, middle-aged man tied to a boring routine. If he became successful in one area, he would have to face his lack of success in all the others.

People like Alan shy away from success for fear of its potential consequences. Their fantasies of power, wealth, and happiness, while perfectly normal, may be a source of considerable shame. Courting success involves taking the risk that these secret wishes will be unleashed. And of course many of us have been taught that we are here to suffer—and *not* to enjoy any success that comes our way.

Can You Handle Success?

Some people find that they and the people around them adjust to success quite easily. Others find that success brings problems in its wake, and may make them look upon their achievements with mixed emotions, even regret. If this is true for you, it could be one of the factors holding you back from enjoying your success.

Look at the questions listed below, and work out how you would behave or feel in each situation. The analysis which follows offers comments and suggestions on ways to change.

Are you coping?

1. When someone compliments you, do you:
a) Accept the praise and feel good about yourself?
b) Accept it, but feel embarrassed that you have been singled out?
c) Make an excuse and end up apologizing?

2. How do you feel when someone you know, especially someone close to you, is successful?
a) Are you genuinely pleased?
b) Do you feel pleased but also a bit envious, because you have not done as well?
c) Do you feel annoyed—they don't deserve it?

3. When you were a child, how did your family respond to your achievements?
a) Did they praise and encourage you?
b) Were you told not to get big-headed, as what you had done wasn't that great?
c) Did they ignore your successes, and only take notice when you did not do well?

4. Think of something you are successful at—your career, a relationship, or a hobby.
a) Do you feel that this is something you have earned or deserve?
b) Do you believe it had little to do with you?
c) Do you feel it's all a matter of luck and being in the right place at the right time?

5. When someone is envious of you, do you:
a) Ignore them and think, that's their problem?
b) Wonder why they feel envious—what you've done isn't that great?
c) Find yourself playing up to them, being overly friendly and nice?

6. When you have achieved something ahead of someone else, do you:
a) Openly show your pleasure?
b) Cover up your pleasure with false modesty?
c) Feel so guilty, you almost wish they had won?

Add up your scores to see how you tend to react. If you scored mostly **A**s, you find it easy to accept and enjoy all aspects of success. If you scored mostly **B**s, you like being successful, but can find it hard to accept others' reactions. If you scored mostly **C**s, your inability to handle success is hampering your enjoyment, if not stopping you achieving altogether. On the opposite page, we consider some of the issues involved, and look at ways to change.

Analyzing your responses

Question 1. How well you can take and enjoy a compliment is an indication of how well you handle success. If you feel you must push it away as not belonging to you, it's unlikely you will be able to enjoy your success. Try to think about what makes you feel nervous when you're complimented. Your reaction to compliments is also something you can learn to change. The next time someone compliments you, just say "thank you."

Question 2. Your reaction to others' success will show how you expect others to react to you. If you are genuinely pleased, then you won't fear their envy; but if you feel both pleased and envious, or simply envious and bitter, you will expect the same from them. If you envy someone, try to focus instead on your own reactions, and look at what that person has that you want for yourself.

Question 3. Your family's reaction to success will often determine how you feel about yourself. If you were encouraged and praised, you will probably be able to enjoy success—your own and that of others. But if you were ignored, it's likely you will feel you can never do anything well enough. However, by working through this book you can change these old, negative patterns.

Question 4. Learning to "own" your success is an important part of enjoying it. You have the right to feel proud about your contribution, and not to feel guilty. If you are successful in your relationships and friendships, you possess a valuable skill, one which many people wish they had.

Question 5. Again, how you react to others' envy will generally reveal how envious you are yourself. If you find yourself trying to befriend them, as if you had done something wrong, then you are giving them a source of power that isn't justified. Their envy of you is their problem, not yours.

Question 6. Whether you can openly show pleasure at your success, and really make the most of it, will be determined by all the factors mentioned above. It takes courage and confidence to allow yourself to experience the joys of success.

You've won…so what now?

The shadow side of success is something many people find hard to handle. Don't allow this to destroy your happiness—take steps to come to grips with the reactions of yourself and others.

Enjoying it!

You should be able to enjoy your success as a well-earned reward for your work, and for simply being who you are. If you are good at your job, you deserve to be promoted. But just for being an ordinary human being, you deserve to have a good, satisfying relationship and family life, as well as friends you are close to. If you are free of envy yourself, you will be able to tolerate the envy of others. Try to accept these facts, even if you find it difficult, as they will enhance your enjoyment of your achievements. So here's to success—yours!

Dealing with Envy

Everyone knows what it is like to feel jealous, to be hostile toward a rival, or one believed to enjoy an advantage. However, envy—where someone experiences painful or resentful awareness of an advantage enjoyed by another, joined with a desire to possess the same advantage—is more complex. The person who is envious wants to deprive the envied one of what they have, take it for themselves, and make the other person suffer too.

Understand what's happening

Envy is a complex human emotion, but as well as being very common, it's frowned upon and rarely expressed openly. Instead, people bend over backward to congratulate someone who is successful. "Let the best man or woman win" is a way of denying that you might feel envious of another's good fortune. That you often feel quite smug when someone who has good luck subsequently falls on their face is also an expression of envy.

The more you can understand your underlying emotions, the better you will be able to cope with envy, whether you feel envious of others, or they of you. Envy is the result of a deep feeling of failure and of the belief that you have nothing worthwhile of your own.

Some people can't let others win because they feel personally injured, as if something has been taken from them. They see everything in terms of winning and losing. Such people expend a lot of time and energy berating themselves for others' successes. They may be attracted to those who are successful, and become their "sidekick"—self-effacing and self-denigrating. This is the stereotypical "yes man," who often envies his or her boss and, given half a chance, will undermine their success.

This was the case with Betty. She always watched everyone around her very carefully. If someone had a new dress, she was quick to make a mental note of it, and equally quick to disparage the dress and the person as much as possible. Equally, whenever anything positive happened to anyone, she was able to find fault. This was glossed over with seeming friendliness, but there was always some sly remark

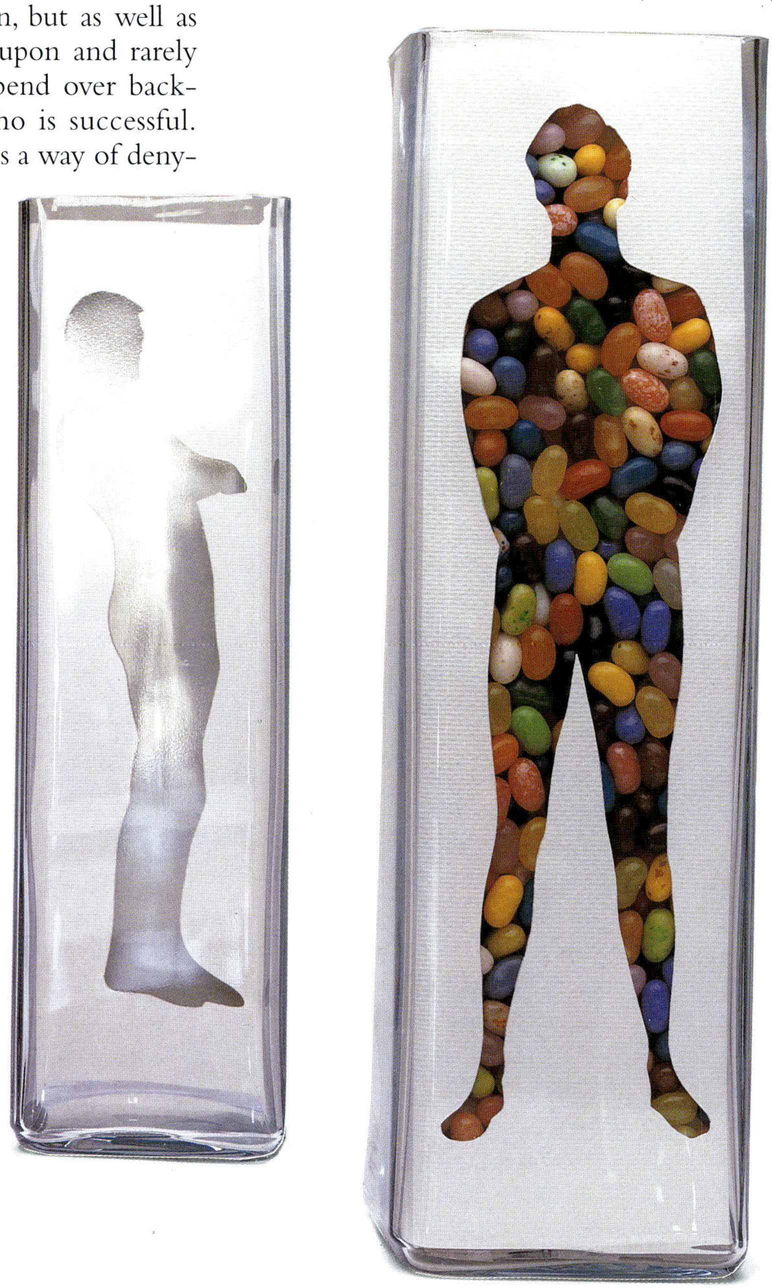

Why should he have it?
The envious person feels empty, but sees the other person's life as full.

that had the effect of wounding the recipient. However, Betty felt just as critical of anything she achieved, and had no confidence in her own abilities. Criticizing others was merely a way of hiding her envy.

Bull's-eye!
It's painful and difficult to discover that you are the target of someone else's deep-seated envy.

When you're envied

The feeling of power that can come from being envied is enormously seductive. It can be very difficult to acknowledge this, as we are taught to be caring, giving, and "nice." Some people can become addicted to the love of the crowd and the envy they feel from others—it can be very exciting to be the object of others' desire. On the other hand, to be the focus of another person's envy can be extremely uncomfortable for both people, especially those with whom you are close.

When Elizabeth became pregnant, everyone, including her best friend Joan, was thrilled. However, she was aware of a distinct shift in her friendship with Joan, who deeply desired children of her own. Although the two were able to speak openly about this, it became apparent that Joan's envy of Elizabeth wasn't going to be assuaged by talk—no matter how friendly Joan was with her, she could still feel the envy as a destructive, powerful force. In the end their friendship fell apart.

This is a good example of how envy can destroy something positive. However, the more the feeling can be acknowledged, the less risk there is of it being destructive. In the case of Joan and Elizabeth, Joan needed help—which Elizabeth could not provide—to come to terms with her feelings of envy.

Feeling it yourself

Although envy is painful, it can help redirect you toward your goals by telling you what you ought to be doing. Seeing someone doing what you really want to do can motivate you. However much you wish you did not experience these feelings, you need to take responsibility for them. If you still feel envious, no matter how hard you try, professional counseling may help you to increase your self-esteem and dissipate your feelings of envy.

How to Discourage Envy

Not everyone—however highly successful—has to become the focus of other people's envy, and if you are being envied by others, there are steps you can take to minimize it.

- **Don't boast.** Of course, you have the right to feel proud of your achievements. However, you don't have the right to imply that you are better than others because of all that you have achieved.
- **Stay "down to earth."** Despite your success, you are still an ordinary human being, just like other people. Assuming an air of superiority can be destructive of all types of relationships.
- **Don't play down your success.** Those individuals who are envying you won't appreciate it. They will simply believe that you are doing it to make them feel better or that you are patronizing them.
- **Don't denigrate the other person.** They have achieved things too—even if they are unaware of their successes.
- **Don't just talk about your successes.** Talk about things that are unrelated to what other people are envying in you. Often, people do not envy the whole of someone else's life, but those particular parts that they see as being successful.

ACCEPTING CHANGE

MAJOR LIFE CHANGES tend to come about in one of two ways. The first is as a result of circumstances beyond your control, like losing your job, or having to carry on when your partner dies. The other kind of change happens because you have chosen it—switching to a completely different career, for example, or moving to another city.

Naturally, change over which you have no power can be devastating—the loss of someone close to you often takes years to come to terms with. Initiating change, however, can also lead to anxiety precisely because the responsibility for whatever happens lies solely with you—you are not a passive victim of tragedy or bad luck.

Take the plunge
Learning to embrace change can open up a wide range of new opportunities and give you a fresh and exhilarating perspective on life.

The secret of dealing with both kinds of change, as with so many other things, is confidence and self-esteem; people who believe in themselves are not paralyzed with fear of what new situations will bring. They have a strong and secure sense of their own ability, not only to cope, but also to gain strength and wisdom from any experience.

Bend or break

Malcolm, for example, was in his mid-30s, and had spent his whole working life as a floor supervisor for a large automobile manufacturer. When losses due to economic recession meant the factory had to close, the management offered either to relocate Malcolm to another site, or to provide him with a generous severance

payment. He rejected the option of moving, and reluctantly accepted the money.

Instead of seeing this money as a financial stake however, Malcolm became bitter, deciding that after 15 years of hard work, he had deserved more. As a result, he stayed at home watching television all day long. His lack of activity and feelings of self-pity grew into a prolonged depression. In time, he found himself drinking heavily and spending all of his cash on alcohol. Malcolm's inability to accept change and adapt to a new way of life prevented him from exploring new opportunities.

Another case is that of Sarah, 25, who had worked as a secretary for the same firm as Malcolm, and who was presented with the same choices. Although she too was unsettled by the prospect of losing her job, she was intrigued by the fact that one of the firm's other factories was near a large university city. She didn't know anyone there, but she was attracted by its cultural facilities, its architecture, and its history. After looking into the relocation package on offer, Sarah decided to take the plunge and move. At first she felt isolated, but she soon made new friends by following up contacts she was given and enrolling in an extension course at the university. After a few months, she was enjoying her new life so much that she viewed the loss of her original job as a blessing in disguise.

Gains and losses

One often underestimated truth is that all changes—even those you want very badly—involve loss, and can therefore cause sadness and confusion. If you don't understand this, you can easily undermine a new situation by denying your grief, and feeling guilty about any apparent ambivalence.

After several years of marriage, Kate and her husband decided to start a family. They were both excited at the prospect, and looked forward to the birth of the baby. When Kate left her job, her colleagues gave a party for her, and several of them kept in touch. During those early weeks, Kate found herself thinking about the office, missing her work mates and longing for all the old freedom of that world.

As soon as these thoughts occurred to her, she pushed them away, horrified that she did not seem to be content with her much-desired new life. In fact, Kate's feelings were completely normal—however much she loved her baby, she had also lost a great deal: her previous existence, her professional identity, and the day-to-day camaraderie of office life. Missing these things was in no way a reflection on her commitment to her child.

Similarly, facing new horizons is bound to inspire fear as well as anticipation. In some instances, it's possible to identify a specific focus for this fear, and deal with it. If a new job involves frequent contact with an overseas office, for example, you could brush up your skills in the relevant language. Even if there is nothing specific that you are worried about, apprehension in the face of the unknown is completely natural—it does not mean that you are weak willed or vacillating. Whatever form change comes in, the ability to take it in your stride, and even instigate it, is an important qualification for success in every part of your life.

UNEXPECTED FEELINGS

When you take the plunge and make major changes in your life—such as resigning from a job, changing career, or separating from a partner—you have probably already spent months, if not years, agonizing over what, when, and how to do it best. This might well have cost you many long hours of making plans, abandoning them, giving up altogether, and then starting all over again. The longer that you have spent thinking about making a major life change, and planning it, the greater will be the degree of your expectations—and potential disappointment. An understanding of the bewildering mix of feelings and emotions that often accompany any major upheaval will help you develop a constructive strategy for change.

Don't panic

It's perfectly normal to be gripped by a sense of despair just before you make any major life changes. This is probably due to a fear that you've made the wrong decision. You may well feel as though this is a make or break decision that you will never be able to undo, and which will have negative effects throughout your life. What you should remember is that, in reality, the outcome of most decisions is a mixture of success and failure. Nothing has to be for life—you don't have to stick with what your decision brings if it isn't right for you.

If you have to make a new start because of a forced change in circumstances, you are more likely to go through a period of depression and hopelessness than if you've made the choice yourself. What lies behind this depression is anger that you're being forced to change without being asked—particularly if you were happy with how things were before. Some people are so filled with anger and grievance that they never manage to adjust to the change in question. Others are able to work through these difficulties and then get on with their lives.

Masking problems

While some people are terrified of change, others use it as a way of avoiding deeper problems. For example, you might find it frightening to stay in one place long enough to develop relationships and a sense of belonging. Perhaps you have experienced severe loss in the past, and are frightened of risking this pain again. Constant change can also be a way of avoiding failure. If you never stay with anything, then you won't run up against failure or rejection. Kathy's story illustrates this. Kathy entered each new job with great excitement, but her enthusiasm soon waned, and within a year she would be looking for another. Her restlessness was rooted in her fear of becoming too attached to her job and colleagues—and of failing her boss. She was unaware that employers were suspicious of a candidate who was consistently unable to settle.

Escaping trauma

Another situation when it usually isn't wise to make huge life changes is following a major event such as separation or bereavement, or even after a positive event such as marriage or becoming pregnant. This is

because your perception of reality is easily affected when you are under the influence of strong emotions. There is a much greater risk at these times of making decisions based purely on strong emotions rather than using rational thought. Even though you may believe that you are thinking clearly at these times, it is most likely that you aren't.

Coping with loss

Bereavement situations can highlight some of the difficult things we feel about changes we have not chosen. Those who have been bereaved often feel that they must get away from the source of pain as soon as possible—by moving house, jobs, whatever. To sit still and bear the pain is much harder, but it has to be done, or the pain may be buried and cause all kinds of psychosomatic problems later on, such as the depression which can come when a loved one's death is not mourned properly.

Change must not be viewed as the answer to all of your traumas. If you have experienced a major life event in the past six months—do nothing! On the other hand, you may feel that you *must* do something, in which case choose small things such as taking short trips away or learning a new leisure skill. The key here is to find ways of satisfying your need for change that won't have any long-term consequences.

Turning over a new leaf

Change shouldn't be used to stop you from facing certain issues in your life, or to wipe out the past. It should be viewed instead as a positive, constructive way to move forward.

Making a New Start

• **Countdown to change.** Give yourself plenty of time, a minimum of a year for most major changes. Procrastination is a common problem, so work out a time chart and give yourself deadlines, allowing enough time to digest the information and changes.

• **Gather information.** No matter what your new start involves, you will feel more confident if you're armed with information; talk to people with similar interests or who are going through the same thing.

• **Don't do anything impulsively!** This is always a bad idea and usually occurs when people feel under stress, or can't bear to wait. You may feel that now you've made the decision, you want to get moving fast. Don't. Go slowly.

• **Consider others.** Your change will probably affect people around you, so make sure you take this into account when making plans—ask what others think and listen carefully to their replies.

• **Pros *and* cons.** In your eagerness to get going, don't overlook the things that may not work, and what you will do if you fail.

• **Use your imagination.** Allow yourself to fantasize about your new life. What kind of person will you be? Where will you be living? With whom? Don't forget to think about what might go wrong, but don't get bogged down in negative thoughts. Your imagination allows a "dress rehearsal" for your change.

• **Don't put off the inevitable.** When the day comes—do it. You should have given yourself enough time and space to consider all the issues.

Reassessing Goals

Many people wish they could change their goals from ones they are currently pursuing to ones which are more closely connected to their fantasies. But they consider those dreams are unrealistic and so don't change. However, even when it's not possible to fulfill your fantasies completely, you can achieve a much higher level of job satisfaction by listening to the messages they carry.

Back to the beginning

Children have idealistic and changeable notions of what they want to be in adult life—a movie star, a firefighter, or an astronaut. Fairly early, however, goal patterns often emerge that indicate a specific area of interest: a youngster who loves to play at being a lion tamer, a jockey, a zoo keeper, and a vet, for example, may have a strong inclination toward working with animals. If this natural bent is stifled—by parental pressure, lack of money, or cultural conditioning—the repercussions can often be felt for many years.

For instance, as a child Rachel loved playing store; she would occupy herself for hours with a makeshift counter, a toy cash register, and a few plastic coins. However, her parents had determined from birth that Rachel would follow the family tradition and study law. Never questioning the path chosen for her, she studied hard and was accepted at law school. All through these years, though, she spent her holidays happily working as a shop assistant.

After graduation, Rachel joined a large firm where she specialized in litigation. Her career developed steadily until she hit her 30s, when she underwent a personal crisis; anxious and depressed, she lost all her confidence. After a great deal of soul-searching, she realized that this was because her professional goals had been set by other people, and had no connection with her own interests and talents. Eventually, she quit her job and opened a shop selling gifts and home furnishings. In the beginning, she worked 12-hour days, but no matter how exhausted she felt, she knew she had never been happier—her working life was in tune with her personality.

Adapting your goals

Not everyone finds they can make their childhood dreams a reality as easily as Rachel. But fantasies can be adapted: a longstanding dream of becoming a doctor, perhaps, may, as it stands, be unattainable—because, for example, you have a family to support and cannot afford to undertake the lengthy training. A job that is connected to medicine in some other way—in hospital management, for instance, medical charity administration, or occupational therapy—may still be a perfectly realistic goal.

Off target?

Many people spend years aiming for goals they don't really care about. From time to time, everyone needs to reevaluate what they want, to make sure they are on-target for their real desires and wishes.

Another way of refocusing your career is by starting to explore a new field in small ways. A life-long desire to write, for instance, cannot be achieved easily within a traditional career structure, and few people can afford to give up a steady job to begin work on their first book. If you have a strong desire to write, try devoting one night a week to honing your skills. If you develop as a writer to the point when your work is attracting attention and producing income, you are then in a stronger position to think about giving up your job.

Most lives are a mixture of satisfaction and discontent. Every path has its own frustrations, pitfalls, and rough spots, but if you are deeply and permanently unhappy, it's a sign that you're headed in the wrong direction and need to do something about it. Once you take the first step, you may soon become inspired to reassess your goals and make a new start.

Reassessing Your Goals

In order to think about yourself in terms of your true needs and desires, you need to ask yourself some in-depth questions as to what these might be.

The past

Firstly, look at your past and how you came to be in your present situation. Is what you're doing and who you are today far removed from the dreams you had as a child? Did you have clear ideas as to what they were? How did your family respond to them? Were you encouraged as a child to find your own way—or were there explicit or implicit pressures on you to conform to other people's goals?

The present

How do you feel about your childhood dreams today? Sometimes people dismiss them, but recognizing your dreams can be the key to achieving what is right for you—whether or not you actually get your heart's desire.

Visualization can help you work out what you want to do. Sit back, close your eyes, and let your mind drift. If you could be doing anything with your life, what would that be? Create a picture in your mind of the ideal you. What would you be doing career-wise? What would you look like? What would you be like as a person? What would your relationships be like? Write down your responses, but try not to judge yourself. Look at your list and think about your life today. Go through each point and consider how far off you are in reality.

The future

Next, you need to look at what you want to do to change your life. If you don't think that you can change, what might be stopping you? Again, make a list of all the things you feel keep you from doing what you think you really want to do. If you are content with your life, and feel your goals are in line with what you want, think about the future—when was the last time you did something different? Imagine yourself five or ten years from now. What is your life like? Are you satisfied with how things have turned out?

THE WHOLE YOU

Many seemingly successful people have important aspects of their lives that they fail to nurture. By ignoring whole areas they are avoiding becoming all that they can be. For example, the president of a company may have a poor relationship with his or her family. To put it simply, the more well rounded you are, the better suited you will be to conquer life's challenges, and realize your full potential.

Get an overall picture of where you stand now, in terms of your personal success in health, relationships, career, and goals, by answering the questions below. You may discover you're doing fine in one area, but not so well in another. These questions will help you to think about what is happening in your life. Then, turn to page 141 for an analysis of your answers.

Your overall health

1. How important are diet and exercise to you? Do you:

a) Try to keep fit and eat properly?
b) Feel that you simply don't have time to worry about diet and exercise?
c) Worry about your health but never do anything about it?

2. If you were under a lot of stress, how would you react? Would you:

a) Assess the situation and try and reduce the stress you were under?
b) Work twice as hard to try and get things under control?
c) Accept that life can be stressful and simply muddle along?

3. If you felt very low, how would you cope? Would you:

a) Turn to others for support?
b) Deliberately avoid people?
c) Discuss things with people only if they actually asked you what was wrong?

Career

1. Which of the following words best describes how you feel about your job and career at present?

a) Enjoyable.
b) Tolerable.
c) Frustrating.

2. If you were unhappy in your job, what would you do? Would you:

a) Discuss the problem with your boss and look into new positions elsewhere?
b) Accept that no job is perfect, and resolve to make the most of things?
c) Wait and see if things improved before taking any action?

3. Do you have a long-term career plan, mapping out what you want to achieve and how best to get it?

a) Yes, you have done it in detail.
b) No, because the future seems so vague and uncertain it would be a waste of time to plan.
c) No, because you prefer to play things by ear and see what happens.

Relationships

1. If you have a long-term romantic relationship, is it:

a) Stable and satisfactory?

b) Unstable and unsatisfactory, but with a few good points?

c) Perfunctory and unsatisfactory?

2. How important are your friends to you? Do you:

a) Need them and trust them?

b) Enjoy them, but feel unsure about whether you can trust them?

c) Have no time to invest in friends, and are not really interested in them?

3. Do you feel you would damage a relationship with a friend or partner if you became depressed? Would you:

a) Try to explain the problem?

b) Feel that you are the way you are, and anyone else will have to accept that?

c) Feel incapable of having any effect on a relationship, or dealing with conflict?

Life goals

1. Are you satisfied by the way you use your time? Do your activities take you forward toward your goals?

a) Yes, for the most part.

b) Don't know.

c) No.

2. If not, what is preventing you from using your time more effectively?

a) Yourself.

b) There's never enough time to do all the things you want.

c) Other people who are putting too many demands on you.

3. What do you think about making personal goals? Do you:

a) Feel you can use them to make your life what you really want?

b) Feel setting goals is actually pointless because too many elements in life are beyond your control?

c) Believe in leaving things to fate?

Picture yourself

If you feel that there is certainly room for improvement in your life, you might want to try a simple, useful exercise, which is to examine each element—your health, your relationships, your work—in turn. Only by building a complete picture will you find where you have a problem and whether it is affecting other areas in your life too.

Flying High

IN EVERY AREA OF LIFE, the framework of success is essentially a state of mind. How you view yourself and the world around you will determine how you set about achieving the goals that you strive for. Set out below is a summary of the ways in which you can harness your mental power to realize your full potential:

Concentrate on the task in hand
Develop the ability to focus closely on what you are doing, without becoming distracted by what is going on around you, or being constantly sidetracked by other problems or activities.

Adopt a positive attitude
Try to confront each new challenge with the belief that you will succeed. People who go through life continually feeling inadequate and downhearted are doomed to fail at what they do even before they start.

Apply yourself
Exert rigorous self-discipline in every task you undertake, particularly those in which you have little interest. Always be willing to go the extra mile, even if this means working longer hours, or taking on problems that do not normally fall within your area of responsibility.

Acquire as much knowledge as possible
There are some lessons that you will only be able to learn by experience. Where possible, therefore, before you tackle a difficult task, absorb as much appropriate information as you can through research, observation, formal study, and qualified instruction.

Develop a driving ambition
Put your specific goals at the top of your list of priorities, and learn to be ruthless by letting less-important matters wait or take second place when it comes to investment of your time, energy, and resources.

Cultivate your communication skills
People who are approachable, good at talking and listening to others, and skillful at dealing with social situations of all kinds have an enormous advantage in every personal and professional encounter.

Nurture your self-esteem
A strong and secure sense of your own worth will help you to survive setbacks, overcome obstacles, and learn from your failures. Where possible, try to deal with anything that erodes your self-esteem: brush up a rusty skill at night school, for example, or lose the few extra pounds that affect your confidence.

Be flexible
Never let your attitudes, your opinions, or your decisions become set in concrete. When new information is available, when scenarios change, or when you realize you've made a mistake, don't be afraid to re-examine the situation and alter your point of view accordingly.

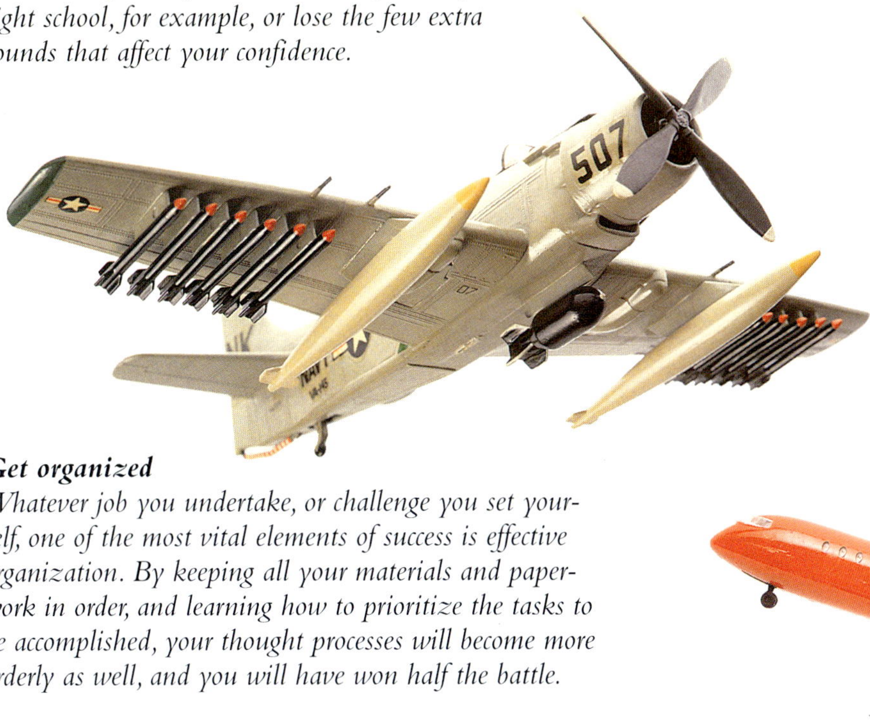

Get organized
Whatever job you undertake, or challenge you set yourself, one of the most vital elements of success is effective organization. By keeping all your materials and paperwork in order, and learning how to prioritize the tasks to be accomplished, your thought processes will become more orderly as well, and you will have won half the battle.

Show enthusiasm
A high-spirited and contagious commitment to everything you do will not only increase your chances of success considerably, it will also enhance your level of satisfaction, and inspire everyone around you.

Safeguard your health
Like a car, your body cannot run efficiently when it is in poor condition. Have regular medical check-ups, exercise regularly, keep sensible hours, eat healthily, and try to limit your consumption of alcohol.

SOLUTIONS

Page 21
Are you self-actualizing?

If you answered questions 1, 3, 5, 7, or 9 with a mark of three or more then you are not self-actualizing. Once you have identified the specific areas that each of these questions represents then you can begin to explore reasons why you aren't realizing your full potential. For example, if you are frightened of unfamiliar experiences and new people, is it because you have low self-esteem or lack self-confidence? If so, then perhaps you need to find ways of building your self-esteem such as those outlined on page 96.

If you answered questions 2, 4, 6, 8, or 10 with a mark of three or more then you are well on your way to self-actualizing. Self-actualizing people are unafraid of the unknown and even positively attracted to it. The more questions you marked with four or five the higher your level of self-actualization. Although this is something to work toward, rather than anything immediately attainable, it is only by working toward it constantly that you will achieve all you can and be all that you can be.

Pages 26-27
Are You Confident?

Mostly As: Your lack of confidence is manifest in most areas of your life. You are probably already aware that you have little belief in your capabilities and fear exposing yourself to challenges. This attitude limits your potential for development and will hold you back from achieving the success that you truly desire. You probably need to work at building confidence and nurturing your self-esteem.

Mostly Bs: Although there are occasions when you doubt yourself and feel inadequate, you try not to give in to negativity. More often than not you manage to overcome your fear of failure and, in the process, surprise yourself by just how competent and effective you can be. Tackling those areas in which you are least self-assured will boost your confidence further. After all, past experience has already shown you how much you can achieve when you really sit down and put your mind to it.

Pages 50-51
How Healthy Is Your Life?

Does the way you live make you feel good or bad? Assess your health by how often you answered Yes in the following sections.

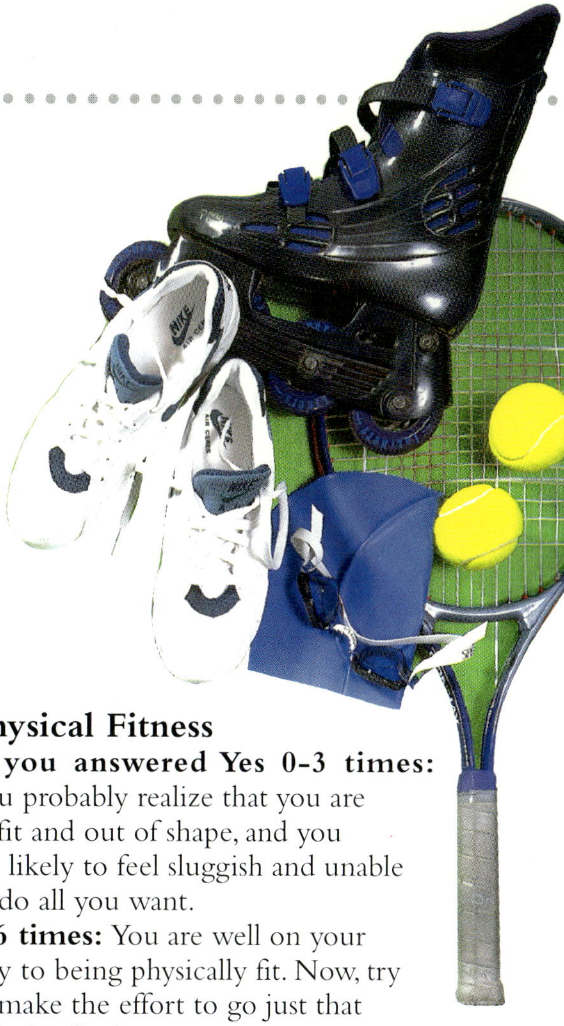

Daily Diet

If you answered Yes 0-4 times: Your diet needs a lot of improvement, and perhaps you have felt uncomfortable about what you eat. You are probably on the way to damaging your health.
5-8 times: There is still plenty of room for improvement in your eating habits.
9-11 times: You are eating well, and should be feeling the benefits of this. Make sure that you keep up these high standards.

Physical Fitness

If you answered Yes 0-3 times: You probably realize that you are unfit and out of shape, and you are likely to feel sluggish and unable to do all you want.
4-6 times: You are well on your way to being physically fit. Now, try to make the effort to go just that little bit further.
7-10 times: You are probably very physically fit. However, it is most important that you take care not to allow your healthy use of exercise to become an addiction.

Stress and Illness

If you answered Yes 0-3 times: Your current methods of coping with stress are probably leading you to further ill-health.
4-6 times: Although you are usually aware of how to keep physically fit, lessen stress, and monitor your health, you do not always follow through on this information, and may slip into bad habits.
7-10 times: In general, it seems that you have an excellent way of dealing with things that may be starting to grind down your standard of good health.

Mostly Cs: Your strong and buoyant self-confidence gives you enviable courage and flair, but it can also have the disadvantage of making you appear arrogant to other people. This need not be a problem if you guard against behaving as if you are superior in some way.

As long as a healthy degree of self-confidence is tempered with realism—together with a similar degree of understanding and consideration for others—it will enhance your chances of achieving what you really want from life.

Pages 74-75
How Dynamic Are You?

60-70 points: You certainly seize hold of the reins in life. But you sometimes rush in without any thought or planning—this can cause problems.

45-59 points: You are dynamic, but you know that decisions need to be thought through to be

truly effective. You don't normally waste time putting off things you should be doing, but you should always keep an eye out in case you start slipping into procrastination.

25-44 points: You can be dynamic on occasion, but you tend to spend too much time thinking about doing something before actually starting it. Concentrate on defining your goals more clearly, and you should find that you become much less of a ditherer.

14-24 points: You probably already realize that you are well and truly in the grip of inertia. There is hope, however—at least you are doing this quiz. You will find lots of useful tips to help you make changes for the better in this volume—for instance, see "Do It Now!" on page 72, and "Making a Life Plan," on page 76.

Pages 84-85
Whose Responsibility Is It?

Mostly As: You tend to blame others—your parents, your colleagues, people in authority—for all your shortcomings. As a result, you don't take opportunities to make changes when you could. Try to see where you are making yourself into a victim by abdicating responsibility, and figure out objectively how far a particular situation is down to you. In addition, the more aware you can become of how past events are influencing your behavior in the present, the more you will be able to change it in the future. Look at "Family Success," on pages 60-63, for further help.

Mostly Bs: Because of a feeling of personal inadequacy, you see yourself as a victim. Rather than blaming others for your misfortune, you feel that everything is your fault. As a result, you tend to imagine there is nothing you can do to improve your lot. To succeed in life, you need to develop a positive self-image and a sense of control over your destiny, so begin by working your way through this book (see "Success and Self-Esteem," pp. 96-99).

Pages 98-99
Check Your Self-Esteem

When you analyze your answers, you will probably notice that your self-esteem is significantly higher in some categories than it is in others. With statements for which you scored less than three, you may need to take specific action—such as getting extra qualifications, changing your hairstyle, or finding a method of tackling destructive or negative attitudes in a way you are comfortable with.

If more than half your answers score less than three, your general level of self-esteem is

Mostly Cs: You are able to take appropriate responsibility for your life, acknowledging when you make mistakes and also seeing where other people may be at fault. You recognize that however hard you try things won't go well all of the time. Nevertheless, you do know that you have some control over how your life turns out.

abnormally low. Nobody has a consistently high level of self-esteem, and sometimes you will feel much better about yourself than at other times. However, people's base level of self-esteem varies greatly, and if your lack of self-worth goes very deep, or especially if it is fundamental to your psychological make-up, then it is likely that it will affect all aspects of your life.

In this case, you should attempt to be more generous and positive in the way that you view yourself, and stop putting yourself down, perhaps with the help of professional counseling.

Pages 134-135
The Whole You

Mostly As: You probably enjoy an overall feeling of success and well-being. You may benefit from minor adjustments to your life, and an annual review of your goals.

Mostly Bs: You seem to be a long way off what you would like to be doing. It might be difficult and painful, but the sooner you begin to review your situation the better.

Mostly Cs: You may tend to have a passive attitude to life, or be feeling generally depressed. Alternatively, perhaps you tend to blame the outside world, rather than questioning your own motives for avoiding change and success.

INDEX

Page numbers in **bold** refer to self-assessment exercises.

BIBLIOGRAPHY

John Bandler and John Grinder, *Frogs into Princes*; Eden Grove Editions, London, U.K., 1990

John Bandler and John Grinder, *Reframing*; Real People Press, Moab, Utah, U.S.A., 1982

Edwin Bliss, *Doing It Now*; Macdonald & Co. Publishers Ltd., London, U.K., 1984

Cynthia Chin-Lee, *It's Who You Know*; Pfeiffer, San Diego, California, U.S.A., 1993

Milton R. Cudney and Robert E. Hardy, *Self-Defeating Behaviors*; HarperCollins, New York, New York, U.S.A., 1991

Liz Curtis, *Making Advances*; BBC Books, London, U.K., 1993

Robert Dilts, *Changing Belief Systems with NLP*; Meta Publications, Cupertino, California, U.S.A., 1990

Windy Dryden and Jack Gordon, *Beating the Comfort Trap*; Sheldon Press, London, U.K., 1993

Wayne Dyer, *Pulling Your Own Strings*; Arrow, London, U.K., 1992

Diane Fassel, *Working Ourselves to Death*; Thorsons, London, U.K., 1992

W. Timothy Galwey, *The Inner Game of Tennis*; Pan, London, U.K., 1986

Shakti Gawain, *Creative Visualization*; Bantam, New York, New York, U.S.A., 1982

Charles Handy, *The Age of Unreason*; Hutchinson, London, U.K., 1989

Charles Handy, *The Empty Raincoat*; Hutchinson, London, U.K., 1994

Louise Hay, *The Power Is Within You*; Eden Grove, London, U.K., 1991

Napoleon Hill and W. Clement Stone, *Success Through a Positive Mental Attitude*; A. Thomas, London, U.K., 1979

Aldous Huxley, *The Doors of Perception*; Grafton, London, U.K., 1990

Susan Jeffers, *Feel the Fear and Do It Anyway*; Fawcett Book Group, New York, New York, U.S.A., 1988

Terry Looker and Olga Gregson, *Stresswise*; Hodder & Stoughton, London, U.K., 1991

Carole McKenzie, *Presenting for Women in Business*; Mercury Publishing, London, U.K., 1991

Marilyn Manning and Patricia Haddick, *Leadership Skills for Women*; Kogan Page, London, U.K., 1989

Richard Nelson Bolles, *The 1995 What Color is Your Parachute?*; Ten Speed Press, Berkeley, California, U.S.A., 1995

Joseph O'Connor and John Seymour, *Introducing Neuro-Linguistic Programming: Psychological Skills for Understanding and Influencing People*; Aquarian Press, London, U.K., 1993

Mike Pedler, John Burgoyne, and Tom Boydell, *A Manager's Guide to Self-Development*; McGraw-Hill Book Company, Berkshire, U.K., 1994

Anthony Robbins, *Unlimited Power*; Simon & Schuster Ltd., London, U.K., 1988

Virginia Satir, *Peoplemaking*; Science & Behavior Books, Palo Alto, California, U.S.A., 1988

Paul Watzlawick, *The Situation is Hopeless But Not Serious*; W. W. Norton & Co., New York, New York, U.S.A., 1983

CREDITS

Illustrators
Gail Armstrong, Chris Draper, Melvyn Evans, Bill Le Fever, Romy O'Driscoll, Emma Parker, Steve Rawlings, Martyn Ridgewell

Modelmakers and Props suppliers
Atlas Models, David Donkin, Mark Jamieson, Justin Illusions, Julie Nelson, Mike Shepherd

Photographers
Simon Battensby, Mark Hamilton, Neil Phillips, Mark Preston, Tessa Traeger, Jonny Thompson, Alex Wilson

Picture sources
The publishers are grateful to the following individuals and picture libraries for permission to reproduce their photographs:

Action Plus *Mike Hewitt* 24
Bruce Coleman Ltd. *Neville Coleman* 81b, *Luiz Claudio Marigo* 24c (inset)
The Image Bank *Bullatu/Lomeo* 130br, *Andre Gallant* 52, *David W. Hamilton* 56c, *William Sallaz* 44c, *Stephen Wilkes* 130br
Images Colour Library 62
Pictor 64c, 128bl, 129tr
Quadrant Picture Library 14bl
Tony Stone Images *Richard Clintsman* 53, *Peter Correz* 60
Zefa Pictures 48, 68
b=bottom c=center l=left r=right t=top